SM

Making the Kingdom of God Your Family's Passion

J. Randall Wallace, Ph.D.

Acknowledgements

Anyone who writes a book should pause and think at some point of a turtle on a fence post. If you saw one, you would know a number of things. First, that's unusual, second, it didn't get there by itself, and third, it's in a precarious position.

Because of that image, every writer realizes that there are a number of people who have helped them during their writing journey. I want to recognize some of them now.

First of all I want to thank my wife, Jacque, for her encouragement and for hours of proofing. There were numerous times when I would stop and say, "This whole idea is a pipe dream." And she would help me with perspective and urge me onward.

Then there are the readers, Dr. Daniel Rickett, Jenny Evans, Jeremy Wallace, Wendy Hammond (two full rounds of editing for grammar…if there is a grammar problem as far as I'm concerned it's her fault ☺), and Joe Oktavec. Each of these took time to read a text-in-progress in the midst of their busy lives and point out areas that seemed fuzzy or poorly written. They helped keep me "grounded" in the real world of people working daily jobs and trying to raise a family. Any writer's fear is to write something that is the cure for insomnia. They helped make sure that didn't happen with me.

Thanks to the Board of Mustard Seeds and Mountains, Inc. for letting me set aside time and resources for this task.

This book grew out of over 15 years of working with volunteers who came to work with Mustard Seeds and Mountains in our home repair ministry for the needy, elderly and disabled in Appalachia. It is their enthusiasm and commitment that I observed over the years that gave me insight into how short-term missions have failed to take people to the next level of commitment. The excitement of the trips too often cooled off into the status quo. I observed volunteers who were powerfully moved and used by God in our community and wanted to help them follow through when they returned home. Thank you all for everything.

Special thanks goes to Dr. Crawford Lorritts for being willing to write a foreword to the book. He is pastor at Fellowship Bible Church in Roswell, GA.

Forward

K aren (my wife) and I are in a wonderful season of life. We have four grown children and as of this writing we have seven grandchildren. Three of our children are in vocational ministry and in a few months our youngest daughter will be a physician. They love Jesus and they love serving Him by serving others.

Recently our oldest son, Bryan, and I were sharing a speaking engagement at a conference in the northeast. Bryan is the Lead Pastor of a church in Memphis, TN. Those who were responsible for the program wanted us to talk about how to influence "the next generation" with a passion for Christ and a Christian worldview and they wanted us to do so against the backdrop of our relationship as father and son. So we did.

When Bryan was speaking I had a flashback. My mind journeyed back to when he and his brother and two sisters were very young and because of the nature of my ministry I had to travel a great deal. I remembered the many nights I would wake up in a motel or hotel and slip to my knees in prayer, crying out to God, pleading that my children would not grow-up despising the ministry and resentful of Karen and me because of the sacrifices they made. But I also thought about Karen and because of her deep commitment to Christ and mutual calling to ministry she shared with me, she had a powerful and positive influence on our children's view and perspective of ministry.

Again, while Bryan was speaking it hit me that the sense of mission that he has is not borrowed but it is his. He owns it himself. I remembered the times he traveled with me and not just sat and listened to me speak but saw people's lives changed by the power and the hope of the gospel. We encouraged him, as well as his brother and sisters, to take short-term missions trips and to love and serve others. And they did. I thought about how we as a family would pray for the needs of people we knew and also how we would reach out and serve them. Somewhere in the middle of all of this a transfer was taking place. Exposure became experience which in turn became a compelling sense of mission.

Mission and purpose in life is not theoretical. There is something to that old line that the most meaningful lessons in life tend to be "caught rather than taught". Karen and I have made many mistakes as parents. I am so glad that God is gracious and merciful. But early on in our child-rearing years we were both sobered by and became committed to the realization that, by God's grace, we needed to be the visible portrait of the destination at which we wanted our children to arrive. That meant cutting back on the "lectures" about purpose and mission and pouring ourselves into living a life of mission. It also meant giving them experiences that would whet their appetites to pursue lives that would matter and count for eternity.

This is the reason why I am thrilled with ***Mission as Life***. Randy Wallace has given us an invaluable gift. I love the way in which he positions mission as core to our responsibility as Christian parents. It is a practical guide to not only knowing what mission is but also how to create a compelling environment to keep in front of us what matters most. What a wonderful resource and framework to help influence and shape future generations! My only regret is that Karen and I did not have something like this thirty-five years ago.

Dr. Crawford W. Loritts, Jr.
Author, Speaker
Sr. Pastor, Fellowship Bible Church
Roswell, Georgia

Table of Contents

Introduction

Of all the things my wife and I have done in life, of all the things we have accomplished, the most important of all those has been to be godly mates and parents. Our greatest accomplishment and contribution to society has been to raise our children to love and follow Jesus. We took this so seriously that we refused to relinquish our responsibility to the church or any other institution. We saw it as our holy calling.

We understood that our job was not to reproduce American citizens, or to train our children to conform to suburban or upper class ideas of what is proper and good. Our job was to instill in our children a deep love for God and to demonstrate that love by loving their neighbor as they love themselves. We knew this would create conflict with the values of the greater society. We also knew that aligning our life with the eternal purposes of God would bring the very power of God Himself into our family. Our emphasis on loving Christ and following Him completely took our lives in many interesting directions and we endured many challenges. Our life was a spiritual adventure. When I talk to our children now, they look back with warmth and affection at those times. Our authentic living, our launching out in faith, our desire to serve the marginalized in society and the sacrifice we made to do so placed God on display to our sons. They prayed through trials with us and saw answers to prayer. They prayed for people we were ministering to and saw answers to prayer. They took upon themselves the burden of reaching friends for Christ and saw prayers answered and lives changed. Their identities were forged in a loving, serving environment. As men, they now do the same with their families.

This book explores one aspect of how to make your Christian life authentic and attractive. It helps you discover that God has a plan for your family. By placing service and mission at the center of family life, you enter into a relationship with God that shapes values and ambitions for each person in the family. What makes this so different from what you experience at church or in personal study is that it requires a greater level of obedience and sacrifice. It involves refocusing your attention from yourself and your family, to God's love for the world. It emphasizes your responsibility to be His hands and feet, loving people in the world and introducing them to the Father. You and your family learn to actively obey God and allow Him to work through you to accomplish His will in the world.

This book focuses on your affections. It will force you to make choices between your thoughts, plans and ambitions for your life and God's thoughts, plans and ambitions for your life. Consequently it involves allegiances. Do you love Him? Are the things which move the heart of God a focal point in your life? Are you working with God in advancing His Kingdom or are you pursuing your own ambitions? For too long we have been content with a mere academic approach to our life with God, a superficial understanding of what it means to believe on the Lord Jesus Christ. Faith in the scriptures involves obedience. Mere mental ascent is an insufficient response to God and His call.

In another way, **this book is about parenting**. It looks at parenting from a macro-view, skipping over the important minutia (which is best covered in other books by other authors). It zeroes in on the responsibility we as parents have to instill in our children a deep obedience to God that governs our every action and aspiration. It places parents center stage as role models and mentors for what it means to follow God with your whole heart.

This book is also about youth. It's about how we tend to underestimate their abilities and overlook their giftedness. It's about how involvement in the real world, the world larger than the artificial one created in age graded education, or in the plastic realm of how youth are presented in mass media, provides youth with a means to forge their identity through meaningful service. Encountering the pain of others and being able to make a real difference changes you. Confronting injustice and seeing how God can use you and your abilities to break its chains, and observing firsthand the unintended consequences of sin in other's lives accelerates maturation. Amusement gives way to meaningful involvement in the world. Spiritual apathy burns up in spiritual fervor.

This book is about new life direction. Sadly, too many people and families who profess to follow God reflect the values of our society rather than those of the Kingdom of God. It has been shown that those who regularly attend church show no significant difference from those who don't when it comes to how they spend their time, their treasure and their talents. Too often minor ascent is given to the concerns of God and He is seen as more of a heavenly "step and fetch it", someone who exists to make my life comfortable and prosperous, rather than someone who must be obeyed and served. With all the preaching, worship services, special programs, and retreats, somehow the powerful message of the Kingdom of God is co-opted by the American Dream.

Truth is parsed into mere factoids; commitment is counter-feited or confused with emotion. Service and servanthood are shackled to the box where "worship" services take place. Too often people react to God's Grand Story as ...*nothing more than one who sings love songs with a beautiful voice and plays an instrument well, for they hear your words but do not put them into practice. Ezek 33:32 NAS*

Since you are reading this book, you must be one who wants to avoid this parody of Christianity and really begin to live out the teachings of God. It is time to embrace a sense of mission in this world. After Jesus died, just before He ascended into heaven, He sent His followers for all time on a mission. For those who decide to follow Him, there is no option of whether or not to accept the mission. It is part of the call of Jesus to Himself. (Matt. 28:18-20)

He has given us the mission of not only spreading His message, but living out every detail of what He taught and helping others to do the same. We are to advance the Kingdom God and embody its teaching so that we are models to the world. We are to do this until He returns.

"And this gospel of the kingdom shall be preached in the whole world for a witness to all the nations, and then the end shall come." Matt. 24:14 NAS

Because the family is the building block of society, I have chosen to look at how families can create an environment where authentic Christianity can flourish. People grow best in a supportive community and families should provide the earliest expression of the community God intended for humankind.

How do you create that nurturing environment where faith thrives? Chapter 1 explores the rationale for having a *Mission as Life* lifestyle. It explores how placing mission at the center, rather than the periphery of life, creates an authentic lifestyle. This lifestyle is not only attractive but fulfilling. Chapter 2 begins to explore how to embed Kingdom values within the daily practices of family life so that faith is nurtured in various ways. It considers how to use the arts in promoting mission vision, transforming holidays into Kingdom celebrations. It examines how to create new family traditions, and the importance of living in a manner which makes you alert to life's numerous teaching moments to deepen you and your family's relationship with God.

Chapter 3 begins a journey, spanning four chapters, into an activist view of the Kingdom of God. An overview of God's original intention for humankind is explored as well as how Satan succeeded in leading humans astray, effectively usurping the Kingdom. It also looks at the plan God puts in motion to not only redeem humankind, but to destroy all the work of the devil in the process. Chapter 4 takes you through the next logical step. If God has a plan and is working it out, what does it mean to you and your family? What does God expect of you? Chapter 5 examines what God seems to identify as priorities in His Kingdom. What do these priorities of God imply for how we are to live in the world? Chapter 6 emphasizes the role of faith in those who seek to live according to God's Kingdom principles. Faith is viewed as a verb, something each follower of God must exercise in how they make decisions concerning their life and how they will implement their obedience to God's commands. Chapter 7 helps you prepare your family for service, providing guidance in spiritual and cross-cultural preparation. Basic issues such as what to look for in potential service agencies are covered. It also helps provide perspective on what is realistic to expect from your trips.

Chapter 8 provides a summary of some guiding principles gleaned from service. These principles do much to help you and your family maintain proper perspective and navigate the emotional, moral and logistical pitfalls which can arise once you get involved in serving God.

A resource section is provided which lists key books you may want to purchase covering topics like the Kingdom of God, poverty, cross-cultural issues, and unreached people groups. There is also a section listing websites which focus on teaching missions to kids.

The goal of this book is to ignite a desire within you to place missions at the center of your life. It's to make it a heartbeat, not a fever followed by a chill. It's to have you and your family make advancing the Kingdom of God a priority in how you use your time, your treasure and your talents. **The longest journey begins with a single step...walk with me.**

Chapter 1

Shaping Families for the Kingdom

My youngest son had decided to move across the country, with a pregnant wife, and with no job prospects. I remember my concern and pleasure when he told me about his plans. This was no small thing to do, especially for someone who didn't like change. It would take faith. He found a job and now, a year later, he was telling me that he was leaving it to launch out into a new career which would involve returning to school and getting a Master's degree.

Yeah, I never thought I'd be heading back to school. The job was just not what I thought. The more I looked at my life, the more I realized that I wanted my life to count for something. Why spend my life working to make some corporation more profitable? I wanted what I do in life to matter. So changing careers was inevitable. I decided I want to teach science in high school. I wanted to work in poor areas and reach kids there.

I couldn't help smiling as I listened. My son was again stepping out in faith. In his move across country he and his wife had decided to trust God to provide and He had. Now, a year later, my son was initiating another change. He was learning to walk in faith, and he was responding to God's higher call on his life. He had begun to learn that God had placed greatness within him. This greatness could only be realized as he obeyed God and sought to advance His Kingdom. He learned that as he aligned himself with God's intentions in the world, God began to work deeply within him, releasing the power of His Spirit to transform his life and to perfect the gifts God placed within him.

Hearing him talk about a career change and the reasons for it was gratifying. He was living out values he learned, and more importantly observed, in our family as he grew up. His life with the Lord was taking on its own character and emphasis, yet in countless ways it still resonated with values deeply imbedded in our family and nurtured through symbols, activities, struggles and teaching.

My oldest son also lives in California in one of the poorest communities in San Bernardino County and he teaches at an at-risk elementary school. I remember when he was 13 and came to me stating, *Dad, I know what God wants me to do with my life. He wants me to become a teacher, maybe a fourth grade teacher, and reach young boys before the gangs get them.* Now he lives the dream. Many of the kids in his classes are children of gang members and he has lovingly reached out to them in after school "hip-hop" clubs and other activities. His peers hold him in high regard and he is recognized as an outstanding teacher. He lives in the community where his kids from school live and sees them and their parents regularly outside of school. He knows he is making a difference in their lives and is constantly looking for ways to reach them, offering them a better future.

I can look at my sons' lives and see that the central values of our family life are dominant in their lives now. If you were to ask people who knew us years ago, or now know us, to describe what the Wallace family was about, they would have said something like, **"The Wallaces are about advancing the Kingdom of God, racial reconciliation and ministry to the poor"**. The reason you would have heard that is it was evident in everything we did, it was the organizing factor in the way we used our time and it permeated our conversations. We served together in homeless shelters and volunteered in a prep school for impoverished youth started in one of the most dangerous parts of Pasadena. We purposefully attended African-American churches in order to break patterns of segregation. It was a source of interest, study, outrage and personal involvement. We weren't fanatical or obsessed we were intentional and focused. As winsome and playful as our household was, we were also intensely committed to these issues. Our kids didn't see themselves as odd when growing up. They thought others were strange for not being aware of what was going on around them in the world and being unwilling to do something about it.

You can see our values by merely looking at our latest family picture. Our commitment to racial reconciliation shaped how our sons dated and married. It also shaped how my wife and I viewed the relationships. My oldest son married a beautiful Hispanic girl. They met in high school and were married after college. Monica is a registered nurse and has a heart for working with poor Hispanic women. They speak Spanish as the primary language in their home. My youngest son married a beautiful black girl whose family is from Guyana (she doesn't like to be called African-American). He met her in high school as well and married her after college. Melissa is an architectural engineer. My greatest concern for both sons when they came to me to tell me they intended to start dating was not the color of the skin of the girls but whether or not they were serious followers of Jesus.

Our sons knew that one of the keys to harmony in a family is both spouses being on the same page about key issues. Both boys sought out young ladies who loved God. None of us are perfect. We are still in process, still allowing God to shape and mold our character, values and emotions. However, we are in agreement with basic, foundational values that help determine how our time, our treasure and our talents are invested.

I thank God for this amazing reality. He truly has been gracious to us. I know that not all of these outcomes are solely the result of our parenting. However, how we approached parenting had a tremendous effect on the outcome. The decisions regarding how we lived our life with Jesus and how we would educate our children regarding Biblical truth placed **us** at the center of our children's religious instruction, not the church. Our commitment to live out our faith benefited not only us, but our sons and their wives as well. Authentic living cemented values in the hearts and minds of our kids.

George Barna states that this is not really common. His research revealed that less than 18% of children reared in churches attend after the age of 20. Less than 1% of Christian youth have a biblical worldview [1]. Only 36% believe the Bible to be accurate in all of the principles it teaches, 75% believe Satan to be only symbolic, 80% believe you can earn your way to heaven by doing good, and 60% believe Jesus sinned while on the earth. For the most part they are biblically illiterate [2]. A more startling finding is that nearly 90% of youth raised in church stop all attendance by the end of their second year in college [3]. The exceptions to these amazing statistics have some key characteristics in common. They tend to come from families where parenting has been intentional about shaping values and where an authentic form of Christianity has been on display. These families place their life with Christ at the center of all they do and the parents take full responsibility for the spiritual instruction of their children. There are excellent books that provide instruction on the whole process of raising children for Christ. (Check the resources section at the end of the book for an idea of ones to purchase). I don't intend to outline that entire process of the spiritual development of children here. **I want to focus on one aspect of that process: implementing a service mindset that embraces God's love for the world.** By putting the teachings of Jesus into action, especially in serving the marginalized in society, we prove to a watching world, and to our watching children, that the message of God is true and the power of God to transform is real. It is through the process of discovering God's truth and then obeying it that our values are formed and reinforced. People are tired of the "fakeness" of Christianity. Our songs about God changing the world sound silly when you look at the incredible problems that exist in the world. Talk and singing is not enough. *For the kingdom of God is not a matter of talk but of power. (1 Cor. 4:20)* However, when people encounter authentic Christianity, when they are exposed to followers of Jesus who through loving service work to transform the world, they are intrigued and want to know how they can become a part of this amazing movement. Visible acts are hard to disregard. How do you go about becoming an authentic follower of Jesus or, what Hugh Halter, in the *Tangible Kingdom*, calls an apprentice of Jesus?

Building family integrity in faith: Authentic living

For too long there has been a tension between being and doing. When we talk about the need to take the teachings of Jesus seriously someone always voices the concern of abandoning the gospel and only focusing on the social. History shows that this is a very real concern, but a concern that is double-edged. In our fear of purely becoming secular and abandoning the message of the sacrificial death, burial and resurrection of Christ, we have fallen prey to an equally damaging error. We have tamed the message of Jesus, which the leaders in His day saw as quite revolutionary on a number of levels, and turned it into a purely spiritual message which has little to do with affecting the world as it is. The message of God becomes good news when both the emphasis on the spiritual and social are wed, as Jesus Himself demonstrated in His life. When confronted by John the Baptizer's disciples with John's concern that Jesus was indeed the anointed Messiah...

Jesus answered and said to them, "Go and report to John what you hear and see: the blind receive their sight and the lame walk, the lepers are cleansed and the deaf hear, the dead are raised up, and the poor have the gospel preached to them. And blessed is he who does not take offense at Me." Matt. 11:4-6 NASU

Jesus explains to John that not only is the gospel preached, but the work of the devil in people's lives is being reversed. In other scriptures He speaks of oppressors being overthrown, those in power answering for wrong doing, the captive being set free. Jesus joins the idea of being and doing into a seamless way of life. He states that you act out of who you are, what you do on the outside bears testimony of who you are on the inside.

When you join being and doing, when what you do corresponds with what you say you believe, you gain not only credibility and authority in the world by making sure that values that are stated to be important in church are actually lived out, the beliefs become anchored in the decision processes of everyone in the family. They become a worldview interpreting and critiquing every opportunity and cultural demand. They become defining factors in how identity is perceived and expressed by family members. They also become windows which enable each family member to see how they are uniquely gifted by God and how God intends to use those gifts in the world. This is actually quite freeing and exhilarating since we are no longer emotionally harnessed to what others say about us or burdened by feelings of inferiority generated by comparing ourselves to others.

When authentically living out their faith, family members quit comparing themselves to their peers for approval or acceptance. Discovering their unique gifts, perspectives and talents through action in service enables each family member to make peace with how God has uniquely formed them. They come to a deep knowledge of who they are based upon "trial through service". By living out their faith as they advance God's Kingdom agenda, each discovers their unique strengths and weaknesses. Each comes to see their gifts and abilities in the safe environment of the family where success or failure can be bathed in love. Each learns to take what skills or resources God has entrusted to them and put them into action to do good. Each person's faith becomes significant in terms of personal identity and social expression.

Far too many people settle for a tame form of Christianity relegated to ritual, rules and religious services. They often define themselves by what they do not do, not by what they do. I'm reminded of the *I don't smoke and I don't chew and I don't go with girls that do,* ditty we mocked in college. This is safe but incredibly boring and tedious. When families and individuals begin to define themselves by what they do, by creatively responding to God's Kingdom demands for relationship with Him and service to the world, faith becomes exciting. Faith becomes an adventure, a way of life that calls to the deep recesses of our heart that hungers for significance, relevance and meaning. People see in us a new type of person, a person who has a meaningful, dynamic, living relationship with God. They see a person who is compassionately in tune with others and who will work to bring about a better world.

All of us, especially kids, are drawn to authenticity. Authentic people often stir us deeply. Authentic people have within them the power of credibility which gives them tremendous authority. Even if we disagree with them we respect them for their authenticity. I remember when Mother Teresa challenged members of congress regarding their acceptance of abortion. Because of her tremendous credibility and authentic lifestyle, none could argue with her even though they disagreed. Her life was a greater apologist for her faith than any verbal argument could dismantle.

Something on which we all seem to agree is that we can barely stand those who say one thing and do another. We all look with disdain on those who talk the talk but can't walk the walk. Most of us do not suffer hypocrites well. This is especially true with leaders. Yet, it seems that we have created a neutral zone, a safe spot, for hypocrisy to thrive. That safe spot is often our families. It is expressed in the compartmentalized way we tend to live our lives. For many, their Christian faith is merely one more spoke on the bicycle wheel of life that helps balance them out and smooth out their ride. It is no more important than sports or proper apparel choices. It's a way to be respectable and accepted in the community. There seems to be a disconnect between what the Scriptures teach, what is espoused on Sunday, and how business and life is practiced on Monday. We state that stealing is wrong on Sunday but go home and pirate video or music on the internet through downloads. I often wonder what would happen if a researcher were assigned to follow around a family and determine, based upon what is observed in action, what the values of that family actually are. How much alignment would the stated values have with the values of practice? What would time usage, spending patterns, resource allocation and effort reveal to be the ultimate goals and life thrust of each family? How would it look for me? Scary thought isn't it? Yet, the Scriptures are clear that such an "audit" is coming in which every idle word and every deed will be examined for its compliance with God's will and His intentions for each of us *(Matt. 12:36)*.

Our tendency to view the scriptures as a series of ideas to be understood and accepted helps to foster this hypocrisy. It does so by removing the necessity to act upon those ideas. We have reduced discipleship to the mastery of information rather than the mastery of right living, of disciplined living. When we shift from an *information* to an *action* orientation, the very nature of our religious belief is changed. Discipleship may begin with head knowledge but must out of necessity move to *experiential* knowledge to be not only complete but useful *(Matt.7:25)*.

Action as the primary means for discipleship: turning from trivia to obedience.

And here is the rub. Most of us are woefully ignorant of what God expects from us. How can we follow what we don't know? George Barna and Os Guinness point out that the average "Christian" is virtually biblically ignorant. When less than 49% of pastors possess a biblical worldview (explained in the broadest of terms) what can be expected of those in the pews who do not have a religious education? [1, 4] Too often the information communicated in church is disconnected from any overall biblical grand narrative or story. What is taught fails to tie into the overall thrust of the message of scripture; what God is doing to restore His Kingdom and where this will ultimately take humankind. Often the information is too individualized or worse yet, diluted into pop psychology or the latest management fad theory [5]. It's as if we were mechanics who can bolt parts together but can't really repair a car because we don't know how engines work. We allow ourselves to be distracted by interesting but ultimately unimportant issues that pull us from the overall thrust of God's message. We end up expending our energy promoting or defending these various emphases. While arguing over marginal doctrines, we lose sight of...

> *"'You shall love the Lord your God with all your heart, and with all your soul, and with all your mind.' This is the great and foremost commandment. The second is like it, 'You shall love your neighbor as yourself.'" Matt. 22:37-40 NAS*

Have you ever noticed that in the context of the Scripture above, Jesus was asked what the greatest commandment was; it seems to be a trivia question. He answered by giving two commandments, the second of which requires us to put the teachings of God into action by serving humankind. Jesus trumped a trivia question with the wild card of obedience. He made it clear that loving God is linked to loving people. Obeying and worshiping God is linked to serving and ministering to people in addition to those in your family or church. Every follower of Jesus is charged with loving their neighbor as their self. Real Christianity is found outside the box of the worship center.

Because our formal Christian leaders have been trained in classrooms, many rely on spoken transfer of information or "spectacles" to communicate. They fail to create activities in which people must learn through doing. We come to a facility, sit and listen, maybe sing a little, stand when they tell us to stand, kneel when they tell us to kneel, and fall asleep in ways no one can tell (confession is good for the soul). If the church leadership wants us to begin to live differently as men, they devise a ten week series on living differently....with appropriate peer stories and macho language and posturing (pastor takes off his suit coat, undoes his tie, rolls up his sleeves and "talks turkey"). Ten more lectures on top of all the others. Yeah, that'll sure turn things around. We are stuck in the fallacy that the mere infusion of new information will provide the motivation to change. The value or quality of what is communicated is measured by whether or not it is new, innovative or novel in its approach rather than whether or not people change their behavior. Compare this with the way Jesus taught.

The word of God in work boots

If you look through the Gospels, it appears that Jesus seldom gave long lectures, since only a few are included. Most of the time Jesus constructed situations in which people's prejudices, values, preconceptions or theories on life were challenged. When He wanted to teach them about prejudice, He took his disciples into Samaria, took water from a woman of questionable character, or ate with sinners and tax collectors. When the disciples asked questions, He answered them in ways that often forced the disciples to think of the issues more deeply and to process at a level which challenged their long-held views (parables can be a pain). They smelled the rot of leprosy and watched Him touch the unclean. They experienced the fear of challenging authorities and standing their ground in the face of opposition while listening to Jesus chastise, or enrage the Pharisees and Sadducees. They felt the exhilaration of healing the desperate and the frustration of their inability to deliver the captive. He constructed learning experiences anchored in the grit and grime of real life. Those lessons learned in this manner had greater impact than those merely learned through the transfer of theoretical information. Jesus wanted people of action, so He took them to places, forced their involvement in situations, and made sure they were uncomfortable. He gave them responsibility and waited for failure or success, both being valuable teaching mechanisms. The focus of His teaching often arose from the current situation, from the current challenge. Each day life turned to a new topic for consideration.

Jesus was really a good adult educator. He knew most people learn while trying to solve problems. They are motivated by the problems they encounter. As motivating as His ideas were, the situations He involved people in were more instructive. From a learning perspective, He utilized more senses and more levels of mental processing through experiential learning. He used conflict to force issues. He knew the preference of the Jews to seek miraculous signs and therefore chose not to give them what they wanted. He knew the desire of the Greeks to want philosophical debate, and He chose to go counter to what they wanted. Jesus did not pander to people's interests; He pushed them toward practicing God's principles.

Am I saying that you shouldn't study the scriptures in the traditional way at all? No. Knowledge of the content of scripture is essential for growth. The scriptures extol the necessity to study them and memorize them (Psalm 119). However, if we reduce them to mere regulations, factoids, interesting moralistic stories or mere literature, we impoverish ourselves. We run the risk of being able to identify various trees in a forest but failing to grasp the concept of what a forest is and its function. I have to confess that one of the things I hate is the tendency to trivialize the scriptures, reduce the scriptures to a series of facts to be learned and regurgitated. The Bible is more than a book of facts to master. It is a Grand Story (the *Kingdom of God*) of how God loves humankind and is laboring to reverse the effects of Satan's attack on His rule and reign. It is full of examples of how God has had to deal with those who choose to follow or ignore Him. It provides insight into the nitty gritty reality of the struggles, the failures, and the victories of people who chose to follow Him in various cultural settings and at various times in history. By becoming thoroughly familiar with this Grand Story, we gain insight into the practical tools needed to successfully follow God, and we gain encouragement and hope about the future of our lives and humankind. This Grand Story spans the beginning and end of how God addresses the problem of sin in the world and its effect on humanity. It provides a glimpse of a time when God thoroughly reverses all the work of Satan in the world.

We need to realize that intellectual understanding of this Grand Story is not the same as "knowing" it, which extends to an experiential level. There's a word used in the Greek in scripture that isolates this: *epignosis*...a full knowledge. This knowledge is gained through action, obeying what the scriptures say and aligning ourselves with its Grand Story. I am continually surprised when I talk with Christians who are unable to explain the Grand Story of scripture, the Kingdom of God. Understanding this story moves us from seeing Christianity as telling us what not to do, to providing us information about what to do and how to live our lives. When we understand the Kingdom of God, its direction and thrust, its priorities, its patterns for families and communities, and its demands on our lives, sense is made of many seemingly disjointed concepts and teachings residing in Scripture. This overarching story of the Kingdom of God (not to be confused with Christendom, the establishment of a religious political system) provides the meaning and significance that we all seek. God's Grand Story reveals each person's unique place within its scheme.

Moving from knowing about God to being with Him

Jesus came to demonstrate to us the person and character of God and, more importantly, that in Him, through Him, we might have communion with God, a close personal relationship. Interestingly enough, that relationship is fostered, nurtured and magnified through action, through obedience. John 14 makes this clear...

*"He who has My commandments and keeps them is the one who loves Me; and he who loves Me will be loved by My Father, **and I will love him and will disclose Myself to him.**" (emphasis mine) John 14:21*

*Jesus answered and said to him, "If anyone loves Me, he will keep My word; and My Father will love him, and **We will come to him and make Our abode with him.**" (emphasis mine) John 14:23 NAS*

Obedience to what is taught, not mere agreement with what is taught, is the key to relationship with God. I am confident of two things. First, each person is created in the image of God and as such has greatness bottled up within him or her. I believe no one is able to live up to the full potential of this greatness without being vitally joined in obedience to God. Next, I believe that once a person becomes a follower of Jesus, the Spirit that the scriptures say comes to dwell within begins to work out that potential as the person responds in ever increasing acts of obedience. Because of the work of the Spirit, our hearts call out for connection to God and we experience feelings of joy, significance and peace when that connection is made. The amazing truth is that obedience to Kingdom priorities becomes mystical encounters with the living God. I use Mother Teresa's phrase, **"We encounter Jesus in a strange disguise."**

What happens when families take this action approach to learning the scripture? I remember when we took our young children to feed the homeless. Our sons sat with men and women and ate with them. Inevitably, my son asks one of those totally inappropriate questions, *"When did you decide to be homeless?" "Did you always want to do this?" "When you were my age, did you want to be an alcoholic?"* After we were done for the day I would ask my sons questions, some similar to what they asked that day. These times became powerful times of learning and reflection. The experiences of the day often drove me and my wife to the scriptures for answers to questions posed by our kids. Consequently, our kids became more interested in what the Bible had to say about what they encountered. I often tell people that being involved in activities like this sensitized my kids to the rawness of sin in its unsophisticated form. They smelled the effects of drug addiction or alcoholism, or just plain rebellion or laziness. When they later encountered these same behaviors in their cleaned up form in the suburbs, the memory of the smell was still with them. They recognized the temptation for what it was and said, "No thanks". They were becoming insulated from evil, not isolated.

However, that's not the most important thing they learned. In addition to seeing people whose lives had been shattered by poor choices, they also encountered people who became homeless because their house burned down. They met homeless children who did nothing to create their tragedy. In talking to those who had been damaged by sin, buffeted by life's countless injustices, and marginalized by the fickleness of economic trends, they learned that these are real people, people whom God loves. They developed a sense of compassion and empathy that peeled away the veneer of prejudice our culture places upon the poor, the immigrant or those of different colors or ethnic backgrounds. Serving these people, meeting and talking to them helped keep my own and my children's heart soft and alive. It forestalls the callousness and numbing effect our affluent culture slowly infects in those caught up in its values. They learned to see Jesus in a strange disguise.

An action-based method for teaching places it in the context of the real world with all its pressures, contradictions, and mess. Context often forces one to make immediate decisions that require sacrifice. The cost of obedience is sacrifice and James makes it clear that only those who suffer (sacrifice or experience redemptive suffering) acquire maturity.

> *"Consider it all joy, my brethren, when you encounter various trials, knowing that the testing of your faith produces endurance. And let endurance have its perfect result, **that you may be perfect and complete, lacking in nothing.** James 1:2-4 (emphasis mine) NAS*

The context places both the teacher and student in the role of learners. In some instances, the student provides new insight that enables the teacher to more deeply grasp a concept or take a greater step in obedience. The act of obedience shapes both, literally forming the way they will think in the future. Character is molded, nurtured and matured by choices. We often worry about whether or not we will act in a certain manner when a large, challenging decision comes along. The powerful reality is that we will be consistent with the myriad of small choices we have made previously. Our choices develop inertia, life momentum. It doesn't mean that we are slaves to our past; it means we are probably going to act in ways we have always acted. The hidden gem in this reality is that character can be reshaped, transformed by merely making different choices.

As a family, we sought to put feet to the teachings in scripture about our responsibility to the poor. Countless conversations arose regarding a person's ability to deceive themselves into thinking their sinful actions will not dominate and ruin their lives. We brainstormed the various ways we can help the poor. We discussed how political leaders seem to only give lip service to the marginalized in our society. We examined how choices we make as people shape us in often subtle ways. More importantly, we had conversations about our responsibility to do **some thing** rather than **no thing**. We examined how we spent our money, our time and what we were doing to make a difference to assist the least, the lost and the left behind. We sought to address each topic from a biblical perspective, constantly reaffirming the relevance of scripture for daily life. Each topic raised forced critical thought and helped shape values in often surprising ways. I remember an interaction I had with my oldest son when he was a sophomore in high school. First a little story.

The brother's pretty good car wash

When my oldest was around 11 and the youngest around 9, I helped them start their own car washing business. With the proceeds they would buy their own clothes, fund their fun activities, learn what the Bible says about tithing and money, and generally learn to both handle money and run a business. This experience had a profound effect on how both sons viewed money. I remember our youngest was a spend-thrift before the car washing business. This changed after he washed quite a few cars. One day while in a store, he asked if he could buy a boom box (a big portable stereo for those of you who are only familiar with MP3 players and Ipods) with his own money. I said sure but noticed, as we were leaving later, he did not have the boom box. I asked what was up and he said, *Dad, I have to wash 23 cars to buy that. It's not worth it.* He was beginning to see the true value of his labor. Both sons became much more careful in how and on what they spent their money.

Much later, my oldest son comes to me and says, *Dad, I want to withdraw all my savings from the bank.* I asked him why, he explained, *I met a homeless family that needs some money for food and stuff and I feel God wants me to help them.* Immediately warning signals went off in my head...I hoped he was not being scammed and I wanted to be sure to prepare him in case he was. I didn't want him to become cyn-ical over one unfortunate incident. When I began to speak,

35

he could tell that I was not enthused and he looked at me and said strongly, *No, Dad. This is not up for debate. I feel God wants me to do this and I'm going to do it.* I was not used to being talked to this way by my son. I took a deep breath and then explained that I was being cautious and wanted to make sure he knew that sometimes people sell you a story that is bogus just to get the money. I didn't want him to make this huge sacrifice and then find out he was scammed and as a result decide never to help others in the future. I also explained that I would help him get his money and meet the family. He assured me he had already thought of those issues and felt God wanted him to act. He also said he was doing it to and for Jesus, not for a "feel good" buzz. He thanked me for not blocking him from doing what he felt was God's will. At that moment, I was proud of my son. He knew that telling me "no" could lead to serious consequences. Still, he was ready for conflict with me in order to do what he felt was God's will. He had courage and heart. We went together to the bank and then to the family. This was his hard earned money from labor on countless cars. My read on the situation? I felt God used him to help a truly needy family in a very difficult situation. I also felt God had given me valuable insight into the life and values of my son. I thanked the Lord for what I saw and for the sensitivity my son had as well as his willingness to sacrifice to do God's will.

By viewing the scriptures as a blueprint for living, by seeking to make God's priorities our personal priorities, we each began to understand on a personal level the mind of God on various matters. During the times of our service as a family, there arose instances in which we would experience a powerful sense of God's presence. Sometimes this was a sense of conviction, as God used some circumstance to address sin or shortcomings in our life. Other times, it involved the arousal of compassion within us as we began to see the people served or situation before us with the eyes of

God. Nearly every encounter stirred within us a great sense of gratitude for God's goodness and the privilege we had to work with Him. Obedient action released the power of the Holy Spirit within us to do his work of drawing people to Himself, instructing us about God, and convicting us and the world of sin, righteousness and judgment.

You can know God's will...He's left some hints

The Bible states that one goes from infancy to maturity by learning to exercise the ability to discern good from evil by practice. It doesn't mean intellectual testing; it means daily decisions made in obedience to God's will. That is what wisdom is, the ability to make proper choices in challenging situations.

> *"For though by this time you ought to be teachers, you have need again for someone to teach you the elementary principles of the oracles of God, and you have come to need milk and not solid food. For everyone who partakes only of milk is not accustomed to the word of righteousness, for he is a babe. But solid food is for the mature, **who because of practice have their senses trained to discern good and evil."** (emphasis mine) Hebrews 5:12-14. NAS*

The tendency to go for information, not wisdom, steers us away from knowing God to merely knowing facts. The Pharisees suffered greatly from this. They were able to tell where the Messiah was to be born but didn't recognize Him when He stood before them. They could explain complex ideas from scripture but missed recognizing God's unfolding plan when they encountered it. They were convinced that they were protecting the faith when they were persecuting its source and His followers. They knew God's words but could not discern His will. They professed to want to radically obey God, yet when Jesus commanded them, they questioned His authority and disputed His directions. Jesus told them they had majored on minors and missed the weighty and true things of God. It is interesting that when Jesus talks of the end of the age, He states that the judge tells those who are cast out, *"...depart from me **I never knew you.**" Matt.. 7:23* Knowledge about God is not knowledge of God. Therefore we must be certain that our lives are aligned with God's story, His will.

Knowing the will of God is a puzzle for many and for some I think it is an excuse to use as a shield from some course of action they find disrupting to their lives. For many years I have heard countless sermons on knowing God's will. Still, it seems so many followers of Jesus are clueless as to what that will is. **I often tell people that I can tell them with dead on accuracy what God's will for their life is.** He has revealed His will, generally, for all those who follow Him. As we will discuss later, His will is clearly described and modeled in the Scriptures and its description of the Kingdom of God.

Aligning your family's story with God's story

You've seen a little of the story of our family. What is your family's story? How would others describe the thrust of your lives and the values they reveal? What do you need to do to begin to align your story with God's story?

When you decide to align your life with God's purposes, you undertake His mission for you and your family. Rather than mission being a peripheral, maybe once-in-a-while activity, mission becomes life. You begin to live *Mission as Life*. The plans and purposes of God permeate all you do, your aspirations, desires and goals. A simple guideline for *Mission as Life* is:

Learning. Our knowledge of the scriptures, its teaching on the Kingdom of God, serves as a foundation from which all our action and service flows. It is also the fountain from which we fill our cups with the "water of life". It is from our overflowing filling of the Holy Spirit, arising from our knowledge of and personal relationship with God that we meet needs of and minister to those we encounter. Failure to take care of this inner life with the Lord can lead us to burnout, cynicism and narrowness. Nurturing our inner life is not enough; we must also learn about the world and the needs in it. It is not enough to become literate in the Word of God; you must become literate in the world. By studying other cultures, learning how to share your faith in different ways, becoming familiar with the different types of poverty, etc. you place within God's hands tools to guide you and your family in deciding how and where to serve Him best. It is from these treasures of learning that He will enrich and direct you.

Investing. Make it a point to free up time and resources to invest in advancing the Kingdom of God. This involves using your particular skills or talents in ways that contribute to alleviating human suffering and proclaiming the gospel to a lost world. It will take intentionality to make the necessary adjustments to lifestyle and focus to free up time, treasures and talents for the Kingdom. A great poverty that exists within Western middle and upper classes is a poverty of time. Individuals in families are overcommitted to what are often "good" things. These "good" things end up pulling family members away from what is "best" in God's eyes. It takes commitment to know that **just because opportunity knocks, you don't have to answer**. Examining how you use your time is often one of the sticking points when it comes to altering your lifestyle to more fully follow God. **There is a fear that somehow you will be missing out on something. Make peace with it, you will miss out.** It is important to put the activity into eternal perspective. You exchange something of lesser value for something of greater value. You haven't missed out, you've merely used your only inventory (time) in a more meaningful and effective manner. In addition to reexamining how we use our time, budgets must be examined under the scrutiny of God's revealed will in the scripture. Twenty-five percent of American Protestants give no money at all to churches or non-profits. The average American Christian gives a little over half a percent annually after taxes [6]. If we were to tip waiters or waitresses this in restaurants, we would be seen as cheapskates or worse. Acceptable tipping is 15% to 20%. Can't we at least match that for the God who ultimately is the source of all we have? What is more troubling is that less than 3% of money given to churches went to aiding or ministering to non-Christians [6]! Where is our treasure? Where is our heart? One measure which sheds light on this is where we spend our money. We need to change our lifestyles so that we free up resources to advance God's Kingdom through supporting not only our churches, but various missionaries and ministries addressing problems in locations difficult or impossible for us to address or visit. It is essential that we change the practice of how we invest our money. Jesus taught a great deal about money and its use.

Faithing. This involves seeing faith as a verb, instead of a noun. It is something you do, not merely possess. In seeing faith as a possession, the size of the faith becomes central to its value or effectiveness. Jesus taught that it is not the size of the faith (a mustard seed), but whether or not it is effectively being brought to bear on a task (move this mountain Matt. 17:20). It is the use of it, the doing of it that is important. Those who are faithing are always looking for new challenging tasks, new ways to trust God and challenge themselves. Since they have a big view of God and His ability to act in the world, they attempt things worthy of God's person. You can't invest in the Kingdom without faithing. It is faithing that enables you to free up time for serving God. It is faithing that enables you to set aside valuable resources for investing in the Kingdom of God. Without faithing, it is impossible to please God (Heb. 11:6).

Experiencing. *Mission as Life* people and families look for something to do… they are action-oriented. They are willing to take on tasks and learn by doing. They want to tackle problems in the real world and take their life with Christ from an internal to an external expression. They want to live out the principles in scripture so that they demonstrate to all the wisdom of following God. They realize that the greatest defense of why one should follow Christ is the very life that fully following Christ produces in the follower. It is nearly impossible to argue with a life demonstrating integrity and God's love for a broken and dying world. Life can trump rhetoric.

This simple outline serves as a reminder of the four areas of focus necessary to releasing the power of God through our lives into the world. Learning is central. We must create a foundation of Biblical principles on which to build our lives. One way to do that is through an action-oriented look at the Kingdom of God. I believe this general understanding of God's purposes and intentions should be grasped by everyone who seeks to follow Christ.

The first step involves choosing Ultimately, you must will a commitment. You and your family are faced with the same choice Jesus presented to countless people He encountered. *Follow Me,* He says, and at that point a crisis is presented to the person. To follow is to completely alter their life's goals, their personal ambitions, and their personal claims to freedom. To follow is to commit to endure sacrifice, misunderstanding, uncertainty, and sometimes hardship and persecution. To follow is to abandon conformity and live authentic, fresh, innovative lives that don't fit into the categories or accepted patterns of one's culture.

At some point all of us arrive at the fork in the road, we all arrive at the river which must be crossed; we all gaze up at the mountain that begs to be climbed. This is how life-changing choices often appear; and rightfully so. These types of choices should be hard, they should give us pause, because they call to the depths of our hearts. I believe our hearts also cry out for these kinds of opportunities. We instinctively know we are made for them.

Summary

Every parent who follows Jesus wants to see their kids grow to be not only productive individuals in society, but to be people of character and faith. This is not something which can be expected automatically because one attends church. In fact, studies show that churches are for the most part failing miserably at preparing youth for the challenges of the real world. Equally tragic is the fact that this failure is also placed at the feet of believing parents who have relegated the spiritual education and preparation of their children to the church, or more tragically, have decided that even their own faith is merely an addition, an accessory to a self-absorbed life which then becomes a model for their children to follow.

We as parents have a God-given responsibility to shape and mold the lives and character of our children spiritually. To do so requires that we first must reshape our own lives to serve as templates, examples of how best to follow Christ. We are the first book our children read. Long before they become literate in the world of words they become literate in the world of mom and dad. The world of words may teach them many fascinating ideas but the world of mom and dad should teach them what it means to live an authentic life of love and service before God. Basic biblical principles of absolute devotion to God above all other affections, the basics of the Grand Story of God's Kingdom, God's great love for us and how we should respond to it, and God's great love for others and our responsibility to them can all be taught and put into practice at ages much younger than we imagine. Having been taught from the cradle onward, they become a foundation on which the rest of life is built and against which competing ideas are tested.

God wants us to live life, and to live it abundantly. When we place God's story as the organizing hub in our life, we transform the mundane into the magnificent. His mission becomes our mission. It is in the context of embracing this reality that we truly begin to release the potential God has placed within each of us. Exposure to no other opportunities, involvement in no other activities will enable us to identify and fully express the giftedness lying dormant in us. It takes the presence of the Spirit of God to release that greatness. It is only through fully partnering with God in His mission that we can reach the pinnacle He has designed for us.

There are many things which we can do to insure that our family is permeated with a sense of the presence of God and knowledge of His Kingdom. You will find that most of these are simple things which can be done without much effort. However, they do require attentiveness and intentionality.

*My husband, our three young children and I attended an outreach event sponsored by **Mustard Seeds and Mountains**. As we arrived to the event we were some- what anxious…worried about the words we would use, the people we would encounter and if we would be able to contribute to the work God was doing in this needy neighborhood. Two simple but profound truths were spoken by Randy – the first-"There is only one Savior, and it's not you." What a relief and what a revelation. The second – "Anything worth doing is worth doing poorly." Of course this wasn't permission to do a poor job, but instead was taken to mean the worst attempt to serve a man in need was better than no attempt at all.*

*Little did we know that God was not only going to use us to reach others, but He was going to use them to teach us. **The seeds of service were planted in our hearts that day. As we stepped forward to serve, we came alive. Doing what God created us to do brought life to us and to others.***

*We fell in love with the families in this complex and began ministering there on a regular basis and had the privilege of watching many of those families make professions of faith. We longed to find other ways to serve the poor and needy. Our family became involved with **Mustard Seeds and Mountains**, taking 7 mission trips to West Virginia. These seven trips consisted of teams from our church, our neighbor- hood, and our kids' school.*

We began serving in a homeless shelter for women and children in downtown Atlanta, inviting one woman to live in our home each weekend until reunited with her sons. Many of the same teams we took to West Virginia also accompanied us in service at the homeless shelter.

Our family continues to have a strong desire to serve those around us. Our children are grown and continue to travel the world to serve those in need. **Mustard Seeds and Mountains** *provided an opportunity that allowed us to do what we were created to do and bring us to life. Rhonda, GA*

Chapter 2

Creating a home atmosphere reflecting God's heart

What do you do when you want to have a romantic evening with your spouse or companion? You think of the setting, where you want to be. You think about how to make the right atmosphere, with candles or music. (My wife and I like sitting on our large porch in the swing, having coffee or cocoa and talking.) Maybe you plan to see a movie or go to the theater. Maybe it's a moonlight picnic on the beach. You go to great lengths to create a total atmosphere which will contribute to a pleasurable evening. You know that small things count, the candles, a table setting, special earrings, just the right wardrobe choice.

Years ago a book was written called, *How to Win Friends and Influence People*. It's still a strong seller and used by countless to promote careers and sell merchandise. One of the central techniques used in the book involves scanning a person's environment when you enter their office or home. You look for those things the person has on display because they reveal the person's interests or values and serve as a means for you to break down barriers and establish rapport

with the person. This small truth sheds light on the importance of environment and visual cues and their ability to
reinforce our strongly held values.

To have a family culture reflecting commitment to God's
Kingdom requires reinforcing the concept on a number of
levels, formally and informally. The values we state should
be evidenced even in the small things in our life. These
small things provide multifaceted reflections of the direction and focus of our family. When you think of changing
your family's cultural "cues" it can seem not only daunting,
but somewhat confusing. Actually, altering family culture to
manifest your commitment to the Kingdom of God is easier
and more fun than you may think. It can involve everyone in
the family and will be as creative as you allow it to be. Your
goal is to create an atmosphere in the home that reflects your
values in the Kingdom. What am I talking about? What does
it look like?

Establish new family traditions

How did you learn to celebrate Christmas? Having grown
up in the northeast, Christmas to me always involved snow.
Many of the songs of Christmas refer to snow. Then I moved
to Florida, then California. The lights were up, decorations
all aglow, the palm trees carefully trimmed....palm trees?
It just didn't "feel" like Christmas. I still celebrated it (in
my shirt sleeves and often in my shorts) and over the years
picked up new "traditions", such as Christmas tamales (the
best made by abuelita Avila), and luminarias. I learned "traditions" can be changed and often for the good.

How you celebrate various holidays and how you spend
your time can do much to reinforce your commitment to the
advancement of the Kingdom of God. For instance, our family
practiced Christmas in a manner that focused our attention
on Christ and His work and followers in the world. Every
year, on December 1, a large candle is lit in the middle of our

kitchen table. It remains lit the entire month of December and burns 24 hours a day. It represents Christians around the world who are suffering from oppression, famine, disease, persecution, poverty or any other destructive influence. Each meal we pause and pray for specific areas around the world where we know Christians are suffering (Christians in Muslim countries suffering persecution, Christians in Ethiopia or Sudan suffering from famine etc.). Most of this information is gleaned from newspapers or the internet. The candle represents their flickering light. Whenever we see the candle, we are reminded to pray for those suffering. This sets the tone for the entire Christmas season because the next thing we do is practice Christmas for Christ. We limit ourselves to one gift per family member (you can set any limits you like). We then seek to match or exceed the total amount spent on gifts for one another with a birthday gift for Jesus. (We also created a birthday cake for Jesus.) Together we determined where the money would go. One year it may be sent to a relief agency working in a disaster area, another year it may be sent to an agency that buys livestock for the impoverished so they can provide for themselves or start a business, another year we may focus on spreading the gospel to those who have never heard. The crux of the matter is making sure the gift goes to the priorities God has declared for widows, orphans, the poor, the oppressed and the immigrant or refugee. Sometimes even the gift we give to a family member involves giving to an agency on their behalf. I am just as happy when I am told that my gift that year was a year's support for an orphan as when I actually receive a physical gift. I know that what was given advances the Kingdom. By instituting these practices, the focus of Christmas shifted from the little red pagan (Santa) and the frenzy of materialism, to Christ and the reason God became incarnate, reconciliation in the world. We still had decorations. We still had a tree (my sons make fun of our little two foot tall "Charlie Brown" type tree). We still gave gifts, but the focus was different.

Can you see the power of such traditions in shaping family values? How will children see the world differently? How will we all view our responsibility in the world differently? There are numerous holidays which can be transformed by a little creativity on the part of family members. Maybe there are secular holidays that can be transformed or co-opted for advancing the Kingdom. How can you transform Valentines Day? Labor Day? Are there other special holidays you can initiate? Are there existing dates on the Christian calendar, which are unobserved by the general public, we can resurrect and use to reinforce our commitment to Christ and alleviating suffering in the world?

Move from party to party

In the Old Testament God initiated a whole series of festivals, actions and celebrations throughout the year to help people return their focus to Him and together celebrate His goodness. Each had their own special rituals and parties associated with it. There is no reason we can't create times of celebration throughout the year in order to refocus our lives and celebrate the wonder and goodness of the Kingdom of God. Having these celebrations especially helps children grasp that following God is not arduous or without fun. Children will get totally involved and want to make decorations, treats or do anything else you can creatively imagine. These activities anchor your commitment into family life and lore. I still remember my children telling me of the reaction of their friends when they shared about the various innovative and countercultural ways we celebrated holidays. To them, it was fun to be different. Plan on being spontaneous! On the spur of the moment make up a celebration with your kids. They'll love it!

Pictures, magazines, souvenirs

What is important is that in concrete, visible ways your family is continually reminded of God's concern for the world and their role in bringing His love to the world. Using the arts is a powerful way to do this.

I remember visiting a family in Atlanta and noticing an interesting picture on their living room wall directly in front of their couch. The picture was large and depicted a group of people on one part of a long dock (near shore) having a dinner party. People were dressed elegantly and it was obvious that the dinner was expensive. The people were totally focused on comfort, ease and oblivious to everything else going on in the world. On the end of the dock there was chaos. A group of people were involved in a frantic rescue of a shipwreck clearly seen from the dock. Frightful wounds and circumstances were depicted. Amazing acts of bravery and sacrifice were drawn with such energy that it was hard to look away. The picture was an artist's rendering of a sermon given by Charles Finney. It represented two types of Christianity. It was a source of much discussion whenever guests were present and a constant reminder to the family of the type of Christianity they wanted to embrace.

We all know art has power to move hearts. In our home we had pictures of the homeless on the wall around our dinner table so that we would constantly be reminded of our responsibility to feed the hungry, clothe the naked and house the homeless. We also had placed around the house small crafts we purchased to remind us of specific mission trips or cultures we wanted to pray for.

Magazines and coffee table books which focused on different cultures were available so that our children would have materials to look at in their leisure. When we decided to start a ministry in Appalachia, we purchased numerous coffee table books about the region for family members to browse in those times when you just wanted to relax and "veg" a little. We also sought out films that would provide fuel for conversation. We focused on films that depicted specific struggles a people or ethnic group were encountering, films of poverty, refugees. We looked for films where people overcame what seemed insurmountable odds to alter some injustice or arise out of poverty or oppression. These films were "faith" boosters.

Throughout our house, practically wherever the eye fell, were reminders of our responsibility to advance the Kingdom and the very real struggles others were facing on a daily basis. These were subtle influencers for everyone. Most of the time, you tuned them out, like we do with all the furniture or stuff in our homes. Our familiarity with them can make them invisible. However, the presence of these reminders acts as subconscious cues, continually reinforcing our values and intentions. As art mimics life, so the art in our homes should mimic our life direction and reflect the kind of world we want to live in. Please don't misunderstand; I am not saying it is wrong to have beautiful landscapes or abstracts. Our souls need beauty. Just as that family in Atlanta used art to witness, we too can use aesthetically pleasing and excellent quality art to challenge others socially or spiritually.

Establish family activities with a purpose

We sought to bring the reality of other cultures to life in our home through a number of activities. We had people from other cultures over for dinner or went to visit them, eating with them. These simple activities seemed exotic at times because of the new environment we encountered, new home décor, new smells, and new food. Oh my goodness, the new food. What fun we had experimenting with other cuisines. (A fun memory is dipping injera bread into a common pot of spicy lamb stew at our Ethiopian friends' house.) When we weren't visiting families of other cultures, we would often pick a particular culture and cook meals they would normally eat. Sometimes I would get a tape or cd of their particular music and we'd play it. We even had the kids help us prepare some of the food. There are so many fun things which can be done that draw the family together while broadening its perspective and understanding.

We looked for festivals to attend which focused on particular cultures. Cinco De Mayo, Scottish Highland Games, Italian Festivals; there are so many taking place around the country, especially in large cities. Each is an opportunity to step out of our "comfort zone" and learn to appreciate another's culture.

Even taking the time to learn about and understand the history of your neighborhood can be a means of broadening our appreciation for various cultures. When we lived in Pasadena, we lived in one of the largest Armenian populations in the United States. I was totally oblivious to it until one day, when I came home from work, I heard noise in our backyard. Our kids were in the house so I knew it wasn't them. When I walked outside, I found three elderly ladies (all at least 70) dressed in long dark dresses (to the ankle) with dark headscarves, gathered around our grape arbor. Two of the ladies were standing on my rickety round aluminum picnic table plucking off the grape leaves from our vine. When I asked them what the heck they were doing, they all turned and began talking at once in Armenian with vociferous hand gestures. After about 5 minutes we got things sorted out and I convinced them that standing on the table was a very bad idea. I got a ladder and helped them pick some more leaves. They left and the next day returned with a bowl full of stuffed grape leaves. My wife loved these (I couldn't handle them). The entire time we lived there, the little Armenian ladies would come and pluck our leaves. Since I didn't know much about Armenia, I decided to read up on the country and culture. It became a source of interest in our family. I found that Armenia was the first Christian nation and that Noah's ark supposedly landed there. I also learned that the first holocaust happened in Armenia at the hands of the Turks and served as a rationalization for Hitler in his decision to eliminate the Jews. Our sons had Armenian friends and playmates. Can you see how being sensitive to simple daily activities and circumstances can be a catalyst for education and developing sensitivity to those different from us?

Dan and Erica in Minnesota shared with me something they do with their children...

About a year ago our family began something new that we incorporated into our evening routine. We wrote names of countries on little slips of paper and put all those slips of paper into a bowl on the hutch in our dining room. Next to that we have a globe. Each night before dinner, someone (usually the girls) draws a slip of paper from the bowl and finds the country on the globe. We spend a minute or two talking about what we know about the country. If we know of war, or starving people or leaders that are corrupt, etc. we talk about how those things make it hard for people to live free and have the things they need. Then, we take turns praying for the country, people, leaders and the needs that people have. Oftentimes, Emily (his daughter) will pray, "...I just pray for the leaders that they would have kind hearts and make good decisions for the people." Eden's typical prayer (at 3-years-old) is, "I just bless that they have warm beds, good food and nice sleep." We then pray that God would show us ways that we can help meet the needs of people in our neighborhood; that God would take the extra that we have and put it to use for someone who doesn't have enough. Our family volunteers at the food shelf in our neigh-

borhood. Most of the time we are stocking shelves, cleaning, defrosting the freezers, painting or pulling weeds in the front of the building. Emily wrote us a note about a month ago that said, "Thanks mom and dad for giving us more than we need."

Our prayer is that we would foster a realization that God has provided everything we need, but not just for our benefit. We are prayerful that through remembering the needs of people around the world and in our neighborhood that our kids would grow up with a mission mindset that will hopefully impact decisions they make for the future.

What an amazing, powerful example of how families can create Kingdom building activities into their family life. Way to go Dan and Erica!!!

You say that you can't think of any creative ways to anchor missions in your home life? Don't worry; there is a kids club and magazine for parents to use in educating their kids about the world and missions. *Global Xpress Kids Club* in Riverside, California has material for kids ages 5 and up. When you join, you and your kids will get a monthly packet of information that includes a global prayer journal, with updated requests children will understand, and a notebook to keep the updates and newsletters they receive. They also get monthly Bible studies, fun activities (like games), a kid's magazine focusing on kids around the world and with stories of what kids in the US are doing to help kids around the world. This could radically transform, or launch, your family devotional time. Our granddaughter Lourdes is signed up and she eagerly awaits her packet coming in the mail (kids love to get mail). I have a list of other websites and resources in the resource section at the end of the book.

What is reasonable to expect from children? Dan and Erica's story provides one level of insight. For the most part, we grossly underestimate what children can do. We baby them far too long and overprotect them. What can happen when we begin to release their abilities? Sagen Wollery, a second grader in Georgia, wanted to supply lunches in the summer to kids who received free lunches during the school year and probably wouldn't have any in the summer. Her mom Pam helped her with planning and it took her two years but she finally opened a soup kitchen at her church in which she and other children (all the staff involved were children) began to serve 200-300 kids each Wednesday.

Prudential has a website with over 300 examples of what young volunteers can do (http://www.prudential.com/view/page/public/11824). The things kids have done to help others cover a broad spectrum. Just a few of their creative projects include tutoring Mexican children in English; preparing bag lunches for homeless people; mending clothing of those who came to a local soup kitchen for food; helping non-English speaking refugees get healthcare, food etc; participate in building homes for low-income families through Habitat for Humanity; persuading the local school district to donate unused food to an organization that helps the homeless; tape recorded over 120 children's books for use in a local domestic violence shelter to help with literacy; raised money to buy toys once a week for patients at a children's hospital; decorated and distributed caps to cancer patients who had lost their hair due to treatment; collected used books to place in homeless shelters; collected school supplies and backpacks for distribution to kids in a homeless shelter; the list could go on and on.

As you can see, there are many ways to turn *talk of* our values into *action from* our values. Doing *some* thing is more powerful than doing *no* thing. Seeing parents cheerfully involved in service or study encourages children to be obedient to biblical teaching. **The modeling of the parent often becomes the habit of the child.** It is important that the activities chosen be family activities and not tasks the parent passes on to the child while the parent goes on to other activities. One of the simplest things to do is to sit and read together. All of us love stories.

Study stories of real spiritual heroes.

The stories a family carries in its collective memory shape everyone in the family in sometimes subtle ways. Stories have the ability to transport us to other eras, other cultures and help us experience the joys, tragedies, break-throughs, victories and challenges of others. From the time our children were little, we saturated them with stories from the Bible and from heroes of the faith. We had numerous copies of missionary biographies and often read them together in the evening. Children learn from stories and they often seem more real to them than they do to adults. In our family, although we liked sports and talked often of them, we talked more about heroes of the faith.

There are astoundingly moving stories of how God has used missionaries to accomplish the impossible with little or no resources and lots of faith. YWAM Publishing has a *Christian Hero* series (a total of 34 books) that is geared for both younger and older readers. They even have activity books. Through these stories family members are able to vicariously encounter problems and overcome them. Through the life of the missionary they address doubts and fears and see how God is able to strengthen. They face danger and see God deliver and face suffering and see how even small, seemingly inconsequential acts can be used by God to comfort and heal.

Through these stories we are able to see what faithing looks like in real life. These missionary heroes are not spe-cial people in the sense that somehow they have some special trait the rest of us lack. They are special only in their determination to faith their way through life in obedience. Their stories reveal their struggles and make it clear that our struggle is normal. Their stories free us from unrealistic expectations and romantic ideas about ministry. Their stories also have the capacity to free us from the siren song of conformity in our culture. "Everybody's doing it" is proven wrong. There are those who go against the current of popular culture and live in ways that are not just different but also incredibly beneficial to a suffering world. Their stories embolden and encourage us. They are part of the "great cloud of witnesses" that have gone before us and left a legacy to inspire us (Hebrews 12:1).

However there are also stories of believers who have done amazing things and were not missionaries at all. They took their gifts and abilities and used them in ways that honored God and advanced His Kingdom, touching lives and building up people as they met them. We all need to hear of people like Ben Carson, a brain surgeon; Cory Ten Boom, in Nazi Germany; William Wilberforce, a British minister of Parliament who abolished slavery; Booker T Washington, scientist; etc. It is important that children learn early that totally following the Lord does not necessarily involve becoming a professional religionist like a youth director, pastor, missionary or worship leader. Seeing people take the natural gifts and interests unique to each and allowing God to transform them and use them to advance His Kingdom encourages the child who has an interest in science, math, machinery, business or film. God needs more than full-time professional ministers; He needs those in every profession, every hobby, every walk of life to minister full-time. God can transform nearly any interest, skill or ability into something sacred, used to make the world a better place for all.

Learn to recognize and seize teaching moments

What all these various elements in transforming family culture do is create teaching moments. Teaching moments are moments in which curiosity is piqued and the heart and mind opened and ready for instruction. Guards and defense mechanisms are lowered; the noise of life is temporarily tuned out. They sometimes literally last only for a moment, but that moment seized can be life changing. The scriptures speak of this...

> *Fix these words of mine in your hearts and minds;* *tie them as symbols on your hands and bind them* *on your foreheads.* *Teach them to your children,* *talking about them when you sit at home and when* *you walk along the road, when you lie down and* *when you get up... Deut. 11:18 (emphasis mine)*

Teaching moments arise numerous times during the course of a day. If we are diligent, we will recognize them. These moments can sometimes be planned, such as Jesus initiating a conflict to prove a point or by purposely ignoring a gentile asking for help. Teaching moments, as brief as they sometimes are, leave deep impressions. Experiential learning involves more senses and consequently is more memorable. The tension of the environment, the reactions of people, the feelings of inadequacy, fear, hope, being submerged in an experience serve to emphasize what is being taught. It also brings to the surface the hidden reality of spiritual warfare we all encounter if we are truly followers of Jesus. When you think about it, our whole day is made up of myriads of potential teaching and learning moments which can be captured by being alert and watching for them in anticipation.

I often remind people that we are in a terrible and awful war. The only weapon we have is love and the only strategy servanthood. Sometimes this warfare involves our own internal issues related to overcoming self-centeredness, fear, greed, insecurity, an overly critical spirit, or passionless heart. Other times challenges arise from life itself. Things fail to go as planned and require flexibility, creativity and dependence upon God; other people's attitudes or reactions offend us and we have to practice forgiveness and grace; we encounter resistance or hostility to our message; we see the ugly face of how evil destroys a person over time. It is these very real obstacles and stimulants that validate the truth and relevance of the scriptures. Real life circumstances continually reinforce why spiritual fitness, holiness, and obedience to Christ are so important. We see firsthand that failure to live in a manner pleasing to God can not only become a barrier to prayer, which is our main lifeline in times of trial or danger, but it can result in painful and sometimes lasting consequences. Those seemingly silly or arcane rules or disciplines we are encouraged to embrace in the Bible lose their irrelevance in the face of very real spiritual warfare and the need to lay hold of the power of God to defeat very real foes. You never want to hear this:

> *Some Jews who went around driving out evil spirits tried to invoke the name of the Lord Jesus over those who were demon-possessed. They would say, "In the name of Jesus, whom Paul preaches, I command you to come out."*

> *Seven sons of Sceva, a Jewish chief priest, were doing this. [One day] the evil spirit answered them,* **"Jesus I know, and I know about Paul, but who are you?"** *Then the man who had the evil spirit jumped on them and overpowered them all. He gave them such a beating that they ran out of the house naked and bleeding. Acts 19:13 (emphasis mine)*

It's one thing to act using the name of Jesus; it's quite another to act in the power of the Holy Spirit, as Paul did, having a vital relational life with Christ and living in a manner that the power of God was not hindered in his life. Paul's life of obedience, his rich prayer and devotional life, his reliance upon the empowering of the Spirit, and his absolute commitment to advancing God's Kingdom and destroying the works of the devil made him a known person in the enemy's camp. They recognized who he was and feared him. In the same manner, each of us individually and all believers collectively should be recognized and feared in the spiritual realms of evil. In this very real spiritual war we are in, we are either overcomers or casualties; there is really no middle ground.

Don't jump to the conclusion that you or all your family have to be perfect or possess the gifts of Paul to be able to tackle real problems in your community or to be successful in spiritual warfare. The amazing thing is that even the most recent follower of Jesus carries His authority and has access to His power when they seek to live in obedience to Him. The first steps of obedience and the first prayers of a new convert mark them out as enemies to those who follow the evil one. Whether you elect to make mission the center of yours and your family's life or not, it doesn't alter the reality of being in a terrible and awful war. By aligning your life with Christ and His Kingdom you move from being a passive target of evil to active resistance to evil in your life and the life of your community. One way or another the reality of the war will be evidenced in your life and your family's.

Essentially, you will begin to live your lives more aware, more intentionally, and more "in the moment". You will begin to "live" life as opposed to coast through life. You will be fully in the moment, sensitive to contextual and spiritual forces. You will be amazed at how your perception of the world will change. Faithing will move from a theoretical concept to a concrete reality as you begin to trust God to guide you, empower you and transform you. As your experience deepens, God will begin to reveal truths to you unattainable in any other manner. Your experiences of ministry will form a fiery crucible which will separate the treasure from the dross in you and your family's lives.

Learning from the example of Jesus

> *Your attitude should be the same as that of Christ Jesus: Who, being in very nature God, did not consider equality with God something to be grasped, but made himself nothing, taking the very nature of a servant, being made in human likeness. And being found in appearance as a man, he humbled himself and became obedient to death- even death on a cross! Phil. 2:5ff*

In looking at the life of Jesus, one of the first actions we encounter involves voluntary self-limitation. Jesus was fully God, but was willing to radically limit His Godhood by becoming fully human, even to the point of becoming a servant and obeying to His death. He did not cease to be fully God; He was not any less than fully human.

In the same manner, we too are to practice self-limitation. **Just because we can do something doesn't mean we should.** As I mentioned earlier, there are many good things in the world that end up being evil if they draw us away from what God would want us to do.

For this reason, I and my family practiced radical limitation in our lives in order to free up time, treasures and talents for serving God. In our family, we let our children know that they were allowed one afterschool activity. This was partially the result of my wife having myasthenia gravis (a severe auto-immune disease resulting in intense weakness) and being unable to act as a chauffer due to her weakness.

Each chose wisely. In the same manner, both my wife and I intentionally limited our commitments to outside activities. In addition, it was made clear that activities could in no way interfere with our spiritual commitments to service or worship. Here is where I believe most people fail. The only personal inventory we each have is time and it is definitely limited and unable to be increased. The same person who decides they are too overcommitted to be involved in community service with the family will spend a day playing golf or an afternoon playing or watching a sports activity at the drop of a hat. Remember when I pointed out that one day there will be an audit of how we lived our lives? How will you justify before the King of Kings your time allocation? Do you think He will understand?

"I was hungry...but you were on the back nine? I was thirsty...but you were watching the division playoffs? I was naked...but you were replacing your wardrobe at the sale?" Matthew 25:34-46 provides God's perspective choosing the right things versus dissipating our lives in potentially nice and enjoyable activity. Am I saying you should stop all activities which aren't "spiritual"? No! Not at all. For most families I encounter, a quick analysis of time usage reveals that the time spent serving God doesn't even approach the time used in other activities. Time spent in self-focused or self-fulfilling activities wins hands down, but the person loses before God. Sacrifice will be involved to bring things even close to being in balance.

This is part of what it means to present your body a living sacrifice (Romans 12:1). Limiting yourself in relation to how you spend your time, how you spend your resources and how you invest your skills and ability does involve sacrifice. We should be so grateful, so overwhelmed at God's mercy toward us that we are eager to demonstrate our love through our sacrificial living. When balking at such sacrifices, we need merely gaze again at the sacrifice of God Himself, sinless perfection nailed to the cross oozing wounds of love. These sacrifices pale in comparison.

A key area of most of our lives needing transformation involves how we structure our lives financially. What do your practices teach your children regarding the money God places in your care? Jesus taught more on money and its usage than He did on hell. Central to what He taught is that we are stewards of wealth. **All we have comes from God and belongs to Him. He entrusts us to use it in accordance with what He has revealed in the scriptures.** He has made clear His intentions for wealth placed in our care. Are we following through with what He has revealed? For too many people, giving money to God is an afterthought. As I mentioned in Chapter 1, most people give less that $200 a year to advance God's Kingdom. The vast majority of those who give more give less than 2.6% of their income. They are not even tipping God for all He has done in their lives.

I knew a doctor, a surgeon, who instead of living as ostentatiously as he could have, lived very simply. He had a nice but modest house; modest cars. If you didn't know him and what he did, you would never have guessed he was a successful surgeon based upon the externals of how he lived. What he did with his money was use it for the Kingdom. He supported numerous missionaries, he spent a year in Africa serving in a clinic doing surgery with no pay…giving money to the clinic for needs it had. He adopted children from other cultures, he sponsored refugees' immigration to the U.S., he supported orphanages. He hosted missionaries in his home, he did surgeries for people who couldn't afford them, he paid for the tuition of young people wanting training to be missionaries who couldn't afford it. I could go on and on. He and his wife made it a point to order their finances putting God's Kingdom first.

Following the example of Jesus, radically limiting themselves in how they spent their money, produced an authentic Christian life and use of resources to advance the Kingdom that was under constant scrutiny by the children in this family. As a result, two of their four children ended up choosing careers in which they serve those in the most stressful and impoverished situations. Another went on to become a medical doctor herself and has a burden to reach the impoverished.

It is important that when you begin using God's resources according to what He has revealed to be important in Kingdom, you include your children in the process. In our family, we required our children from an early age to not only tithe their allowances or earned income, but to develop an attitude of spontaneous response to the Holy Spirit's prompting to make special donations to causes or issues dear to the heart of God. These were to be above and beyond their regular giving. The habits your children develop in the home will be the ones they enact later. I now see my own sons enacting the same values in their households.

By limiting ourselves, we free up time for all of us to first of all, just do family things together like eat meals with one another, spend time together in the evening, and study scripture together. It also freed up time to minister together since we didn't have multiple demands on our time.

Place learning the Word of God as a priority for family members

Psalm 119 is nestled in the exact center of the Bible; accident or divine intent? The entire focus of the Psalm is the preeminence of the Word of God in the life of those who follow God and the benefits of memorizing it, reflecting upon it, and obeying it. Being students of the Word of God is crucial. **God reveals Himself and His master plan in His Word.** Regular, systematic reading of His Word is the minimum that should be expected of every family member who is able to read. A parent reading the scriptures to children provides a whole new level of quality time. Truly reading His Word involves more than looking at a verse or two every day. Our lives are so hectic, so full of demands, concerns, and fears that it is possible to read small portions and never really see or hear what it says since our minds are too preoccupied. Reading small portions alone also keeps us from getting the big picture. **We must intentionally set aside time to be still and allow the Holy Spirit to speak to us.** For many, this alone is a radical change and takes time to fully implement. However, if we are serious about aligning our lives with the desires of God, we must become familiar with what God's desires are.

It is also important that we do not substitute devotional writings for reading God's Word. Devotional writings are a good supplement and useful for prodding our imagination, but they do not possess the special power God has placed upon His Word to transform and do not have the promise God has placed upon His Word's ability to accomplish His goals (Isa. 55:11). Families should have times together when the focus is God's Word. Reading it, discussing it, pondering it, and just enjoying it. Check it out: God cares not one iota for excuses about why communing in His Word is avoided. An excuse is a skin of a reason stuffed with a lie. Being anchored in God's Word is the most basic of disciplines. It is foundational for everything that follows.

Summary

Creating a family culture of Kingdom living and mission involves cascading layers of visual, informational, artistic, and experiential activities. Holidays can be co-opted and "redeemed" for advancing God's Kingdom. Art in every form can reinforce our values and dreams for the world. Nearly every daily activity holds with it teaching moments in which values can be explored and probing questions asked regarding God's purposes in the world.

Above all, this can be fun. By being creative, deep truths can be packaged in a manner that enables even small children to understand and respond in obedience. This creative reorientation of family culture can be a truly family activity, with each member, regardless of age, contributing a key activity or element.

Central to providing a family culture that supports missions is self-limitation, a restructuring of time and resources to emphasize things dear to God's heart, things which advance His Kingdom. How our time and resources are used communicate our true values. How intentional are you in using your leisure time, your money, or your talents?

Our church here (Grace Gathering) **encourages us to make ministry a way of life.** *Instead of having a few people in charge of various ministries, the body itself is challenged to be the hands and feet of Christ in our communities.* **Dozens of "house churches" have their own, specific missional focus, and they work (single house churches or as a group of house churches) to spread the Gospel to the "least of these." There are groups who minister to the elderly, to youth, to Burmese refugees, to special-needs individuals and their families, to those in (or recently released from) jail, to men struggling with addictions, to unwed mothers, etc.** *In this way, we have been challenged to go out and do the work of the Kingdom instead of expecting "somebody at the church" to do so. We are challenged to build relationships in three directions: up (with God), in (with fellow believers), and especially out (with the "least of these"). It has been exciting to hear the stories of how God has used these small groups to shine Light into dark places. In coming alongside these various "least," people are encountering Jesus. Lonnilea, MN*

Chapter 3

Helping your family learn about God's Kingdom

Whenever a person comes to follow Jesus, they know-ingly, or unknowingly, choose at that moment to begin to align their lives with God's purpose in His story... history. Unfortunately, for many of those same followers, no one takes the time to help them understand what God's story is, the significance and implications of redemption in that story, and how that story will be ultimately played out in the future. It is interesting that Jesus taught about the Kingdom of God throughout His whole ministry. He used two terms to refer to it, the kingdom of heaven and kingdom of God.

> *Then Jesus said to his disciples, "Truly I tell you, it is hard for the rich to enter the **kingdom of heaven**. Again I tell you, it is easier for a camel to go through the eye of a needle than for the rich to enter the **kingdom of God**." Matt. 19:23 (emphasis mine)*

Some of Jesus' most significant conflicts and His harshest criticisms centered around misunderstandings leaders of the day and common people had of God's purpose and plan for establishing His Kingdom and its consequent effect on daily living. Jesus came to initiate the Kingdom and recruit followers who would embody His principles in daily living. Within this Kingdom message, this declaration of God's purposes and intentions for humankind, resides the whole of scriptural teaching. When scripture is divorced from this story, this grand design, and taught as mere facts or commands to follow, it becomes what seem to be collections of arbitrary rules, optional, eccentric prescriptives or lifestyle pronouncements producing a lifeless adherence to duty for duty's sake. It's boring, tedious, and just plain pointless for many when compared to the smorgasbord of alternate lifestyles promoted in our popular culture. The concept of the Kingdom is hard for those raised in a democratic republic to grasp. We are used to having a say in what we do, we do not understand the concept of sovereignty. To understand the Kingdom of God, we must understand that first, it is the King's domain. It essentially is where the King reigns. We are His subjects and His will supersedes our will.

However, I have found that when people begin to grasp God's intentions for humanity and understand that He created within each person greatness and endowed them with tremendous and unique gifts; when they understand how God intends to use them to shape their communities and construct a future and a world which is attractive for living and upholds our highest ideals; an excitement grows within them, they resonate with the potential to construct a fulfilling life. They compare their individual dreams for life with this glorious life God offers and their hearts are captured by God's love. They come to realize that they have encountered a treasure which had been hidden, a gem which had been overlooked, and that they have the opportunity to completely possess it. What does this Kingdom look like? What does it require of me and you? How must you embody its values and fulfill its demands?

God's original intention for humankind

When you look at man and woman in the Garden of Eden in Genesis, just after God created them, you discover the seeds of God's intention for humankind. They had communion with God, they experienced a loving relationship with one another, and they had meaningful work that supplied all they needed for daily life. They lived in a virtual paradise, a peaceful setting. This was part of the King's dominion (God's rule), His Kingdom. This early section of Genesis presents the first look at how God intended people to live in relation to Him, His creation and with one another. The dominant themes of harmony, meaning, significance through work, security, community, and relationship with God are present. These same images were used later in scripture to typify what God ultimately referred to as Shalom, the word translated peace through most of the Old Testament. Peace in this context meant more than merely an absence from conflict (although that is certainly included); it inferred a state of total harmony and well- being physically, spiritually, socially, emotionally, psychologically, economically and politically. Just a few passages draw attention to how peace is used in both testaments to embrace the Kingdom of God (highlighting in passages is mine for emphasis).

*"He will judge between many peoples and will settle disputes for strong nations far and wide. **They will beat their swords into plowshares and their spears into pruning hooks. Nation will not take up sword against nation, nor will they train for war anymore. Everyman will sit under his own vine and under his own fig tree, and no one will make them afraid***

for the Lord Almighty has spoken." Micah 4:3
(emphasis mine)

Each person would sit under their own vine and their own fig tree, weapons of war converted to food production. This is a symbol of economic security and social harmony. It is a freedom from fear of war or conflict. It is a fuller meaning of peace, shalom, freedom not only from war, but the security of economic, social and domestic tranquility.

"During Solomon's lifetime, Judah and Israel, from Dan to Beersheba lived in safety, each man under his own vine and fig tree." 1 Kings 4:25 *(emphasis mine)*

It is also captures the work of God's Son, Jesus, who comes to help restore the peace of God initiated in the Garden of Eden. Christ comes to create peace between God and humankind as well as between people in their various expressions of conflict with one another.

*"For He Himself is our **peace**, who has made the two one and destroyed the barrier, the dividing wall of hostility, by abolishing in His flesh the law with its commandments and regulations. His purpose was to create in Himself one new man out of the two, thus making peace, and in this one body to put to death their hostility. **He came and preached peace to you who were far away and peace to those who were near."** Eph. 2:14-17 (emphasis mine)*

God's intentions for humankind did not include war, famine, strife, disease, drudgery, conflict, or any of the other myriad of conditions with which we struggle and which seek to crush our lives or spirits and which rob us of joy and peace. God made humans to be with Him and deep within us our hearts cry out for the fulfillment which can only come from that relationship. All other disappointments, challenges, and sufferings are secondary to that reality for it alone speaks to the depth of our person, the bedrock of our identity. God reigns whether or not we enjoy relationship with Him and regardless of whether we recognize the existence of His Kingdom. His Kingdom is here, and it is active. Some have sought to put the reality of God's reign somewhere in the future but the scriptures use language which can't be mistaken.

God's Kingdom is present now

When Paul speaks to the Thessalonians, he encourages them that their suffering is for the Kingdom of God, a present reality.

> *"All this is evidence that God's judgment is right, and as a result you will be counted worthy of the **Kingdom of God, for which you are suffering.**" II Thess. 1:5 (emphasis mine)*

Jesus informs those who looked for some future inauguration of the Kingdom, as some political system, to look no further. The Kingdom of God is present in a more universal form. It is not Christendom, some political theocracy headed by a titular head either selected by people or grasping position by coercion. The Kingdom of God is a living reality of God's reign in the hearts of people.

> *"The kingdom of God does not come with your careful observation, nor will people say, "Here it is!", or "There it is!", **because the Kingdom of God is within you.**" Luke 17:21 (emphasis mine)*

The Kingdom of God exists in present reality wherever the feet of those who follow Jesus walk. The Kingdom of God begins first with a relationship with God, Christ living in you and you pledging your unyielding allegiance and obedience to Him. Then you begin to experientially realize His Kingdom's existence. It is present where no one acknowledges the existence of God or where no churches or followers exist. Since the Kingdom of God involves the spiritual, versus political, reign of God, it is eternal and consequently permeates the universe residing as unrealized potential to many.

The Kingdom of God will ultimately come to full fruition in the future

The gloriousness of that Kingdom is explained in the book of Isaiah in many places. One of the greater passages is in Isaiah 61, a passage quoted by Jesus to inaugurate His ministry and to alert all to the reality of the Kingdom's presence. What would happen in the current world when the Kingdom fully comes to fruition?

The Spirit of the Sovereign LORD is on me, because the LORD has anointed me to proclaim good news to the poor. He has sent me to bind up the brokenhearted, to proclaim freedom for the captives and release from darkness for the prisoners, to proclaim the year of the LORD's favor and the day of vengeance of our God, to comfort all who mourn, and provide for those who grieve in Zion— to bestow on them a crown of beauty instead of ashes, the oil of joy instead of mourning, and a garment of praise instead of a spirit of despair. They will be called mighty oaks, a planting of the LORD for the display of his splendor. Isa. 61:1

They will rebuild the ancient ruins and restore the places long devastated; they will renew the ruined

73

cities that have been devastated for generations.
Strangers will shepherd your flocks; foreigners will
work your fields and vineyards. And you will be called
priests of the LORD, you will be named ministers of
our God. You will feed on the wealth of nations, and
in their riches you will boast. Isa. 61:4

Wow!! The images contained in the passage are emotionally powerful. It calls deeply to our hearts and our hearts resonate with its message. We know we were made for more than the mundane. God intended us to be with Him and assist Him in the world.

God intended that all humankind would be aware of His original intentions and of how life could truly be lived when in relationship with Him. There will come a day when the knowledge of God will fill the whole earth. Until that time, it is His will that we proclaim the reality of His Kingdom living out its principles so all in the world can see what it truly means to be a follower of God. Jesus taught that the good news of the Kingdom must be declared to all people's (ethnic groups) before God would finally bring about its complete expression.

And this gospel of the kingdom will be preached in
the whole world as a testimony to all nations, and
then the end will come. Matt. 24:14

Yet, it remains somewhat of a mystery. A major reason is that not all people care about the Kingdom or about the one true God. Consequently, when Jesus taught, He veiled his language, knowing that those who were ready to hear, whose hearts were already seeking, would continue to pursue and eventually grasp His message. When asked why He veiled His message, Jesus answered,

*...The knowledge of the secrets of the kingdom
of heaven has been given to you, but not to them.
Those who have will be given more, and they will
have an abundance. As for those who do not have,
even what they have will be taken from them. **This is
why I speak to them in parables:** "Though seeing,
they do not see; though hearing, they do not hear or
understand. In them is fulfilled the prophecy of Isaiah:
" 'You will be ever hearing but never understanding;
you will be ever seeing but never perceiving. For this
people's heart has become calloused; they hardly
hear with their ears, and they have closed their eyes.
Matt. 13:11ff (emphasis mine)*

If the Kingdom is so wonderful and life with God is so
great, why don't people want to follow Him? If God originally set in motion an idyllic life, what happened that got
things so messed up?

The Kingdom Usurped; Satan attacks people to get back at God

The world is in a mess because Satan sought to usurp
leadership in God's Kingdom and destroy what God had
declared to be good. Satan's whole purpose was to destroy
everything dear to God. His attack was subtle and brilliant.
Rather than immediately coerce humankind to blatantly disobey God, he first sought to undermine their confidence in
God, to plant doubts within them that following God was not
really in their best interest. Look at how Satan manipulates
humans, isolating the greatness God placed within them as a
potential for corruption.

*Now **the serpent was more crafty** than any of the
wild animals the LORD God had made. He said to
the woman, "Did God really say, 'You must not eat*

from any tree in the garden?'" The woman said to the serpent, "We may eat fruit from the trees in the garden, but God did say, 'You must not eat fruit from the tree that is in the middle of the garden, and you must not touch it, or you will die.'" Gen 3:1

"You will not certainly die," the serpent said to the woman **"For God knows that when you eat of it your eyes will be opened, and you will be like God, knowing good and evil." *Gen. 3:4***

When the woman saw that the fruit of the tree was good for food and pleasing to the eye, and also desirable for gaining wisdom, she took some and ate it. She also gave some to her husband, who was with her, and he ate it. Then the eyes of both of them were opened, and they realized they were naked; so they sewed fig leaves together and made coverings for themselves. Then the man and his wife heard the sound of the LORD God as he was walking in the garden in the cool of the day, and **they hid from the LORD God among the trees of the garden***. Gen. 3:6*

Satan not only sought to have people sin, but to have them become suspicious and afraid of God. Satan himself was cast out of heaven for wanting to be like God (Ezek. 28:11-19 and Isa. 14: 12-25). Satan then tempts humankind with the same desire, built on the same premise *"...you can only fulfill your full potential apart from God.* **God doesn't desire the best for you***, He desires to hold you back."* By planting this initial doubt, all else follows, leading eventually to a fear of God and desire to live apart from Him. People feel God can't be trusted, and they are on their own. Since God can't be trusted, you cannot really trust anyone.

Consequently, any manifestation of community is fractured by suspicion, blame, irresponsibility, and conflict. From this point on, humankind is distrustful of any expression of God and fearful of the implications of acknowledging any presence of God. Because there is no relationship or fellowship with God, humans are cast upon a sea of self-interest and relativity struggling to make sense of life and yearning for more than what they are experiencing. Humans sail for what they hope are more fulfilling shores while bereft of any compass, using only their senses and imagination for navigation, all the while denying they are hopelessly lost.

This quest for knowledge of good apart from God throws all creation into crisis and effectively places Satan as the defacto "god of this world". Satan's hope was to steal away the crown of God's creation and have humans serve him, the ultimate affront to God. However, rather than openly serve Satan, humans chose for the most part to serve themselves, making their dreams and desires their idols. From these decisions by Adam and Eve flow all the despicable practices present in every human heart and culture. Every crime, illness, war, degenerate act, exploitation, oppression and misery known to humankind finds as its source this decision to live apart from God, to live according to our own standards, defining good and evil for ourselves. The Kingdom of God, at least on the surface, is usurped and all creation is no longer in service to God and subject to His will.

The Kingdom Strikes Back

The whole rest of scripture provides an account of how God in His foreknowledge, from the foundation of the world, put in motion a plan to restore His Kingdom and deal with the sin issue, redeeming humankind, once and for all. He put His knowledge on display to the universe and His love in action. Ephesians puts it this way...

> *...make plain to everyone the administration of this mystery, which for ages past was kept hidden in God, who created all things.* **His intent was that now, through the church, the manifold wisdom of God should be made known to the rulers and authorities in the heavenly realms, according to his eternal purpose that he accomplished in Christ Jesus our Lord.** *In him and through faith in him we may approach God with freedom and confidence. Eph. 3:8ff (emphasis mine)*

It is through Christ that God regains humankind's trust. He demonstrates that He is indeed looking out for our best interests and that ultimately, we find satisfaction, fulfillment and meaning only in relationship with Him. His quest to restore His Kingdom culminates in the death, burial and resurrection of Jesus. The path to this summit winds through the entire Old Testament.

God has to convince people of His good intentions and that life apart from Him is little more than a taste of hell on earth. To do this, He begins a series of relationships with different people throughout history, using each one to give a little better picture of Himself and setting in motion a plan to provide a working model, a demonstration of what His Kingdom would be like once people followed Him. Each story in the Old Testament is a window into God's character, nature and plans. Each story provides another facet of insight into how life apart from God is distorted in some manner and how God must deal with it.

A key person is Abraham in Genesis 12. By focusing on an individual, God reveals how important each person is in His eyes and emphasizes how one person's life that follows God can have repercussions throughout history.

*I will make you into a great nation and **I will bless
you**; I will make your name great, and you will be
a blessing. I will bless those who bless you, and
whoever curses you I will curse; and **all peoples on
earth will be blessed through you**. Gen. 12:2-32*

By choosing Abraham, God also begins to reveal how
a family following God can have amazing impact in the
world (it is Abraham's family through which God unfolds
His divine plan). His relationship with Abraham allows God
to slowly reveal His plans for people and their role in the
world. As he told Abraham, **God blesses us in order that
we might be a blessing to others.** Later, when speaking
to Moses in Exodus, He begins to forge a people who will
reveal to the world His Kingdom principles.

*Now if you obey me fully and keep my covenant, then
out of all nations you will be my treasured possession. Although the whole earth is mine, **you will be
for me a kingdom of priests and a holy nation**.' Ex.
19:5 (emphasis mine)*

The children of Israel were to be witnesses not only of
God's greatness, they were also to embody His principles
of living in order for the world to see His original intentions for humankind. By living out God's principles in their
daily lives and government, the rest of the world should be
able to look at the Israelites individually and as a people and
understand not only what it meant to trust in God and follow
Him, but to see how much better life would be if they did.
This same theme is carried over into the New Testament.
Followers of Jesus were expected to live in a manner that put
God on display and demonstrated to the world the wisdom of
following God. We are called God's chosen people, a priesthood, a holy nation.

But you are a chosen people, a royal priesthood, a holy nation, God's special possession, that you may declare the praises of him who called you out of darkness into his wonderful light. Once you were not a people, but now you are the people of God; once you had not received mercy, but now you have received mercy. 1Pe. 2:9 (emphasis mine)

We are to live in such a way that people see us as being very different from the average person. Our lives should enable people to see what God is like; we are a window into the heart of God for those around us. We act as a contact point, a ground of introduction between a world hostile toward God, and God, who loves the world. We are the priests, the go-betweens who introduce people to God and go before Him (in intercessory prayer) on their behalf. The way we live should disarm people, challenge their misconceptions about God and neutralize their hostility through kindness and love. Our lives demonstrate that through Christ's sacrifice and our relationship with Him we can gain power over sin. Because of Christ's sacrifice, we can be free from the consequences of sin in our personal lives, our families, our neighborhood and community. God's values should permeate our lives and the social institutions that arise from our life on earth.

God revealed a great deal about how we, as a people of God, are to live in the world. It's important to remember that when God approaches Moses, thousands of years of human history has already passed. Humans have developed ways of living, ways of relating to others, and social institutions which embody life without God. So, when God sets forth His agenda for being a people of God, He must address many of those negative and destructive traditions.

When He used Moses to call out the children of Israel from bondage in Egypt, He established laws that revealed

His character and the principles of His Kingdom. Anchored within those laws were correctives which would serve to counter the innate self-centeredness of people and their tendency to oppress others and create unjust systems. These can be read about in Leviticus 25 and Deuteronomy 15. Some of the most significant involve the forgiveness of debts every seven years and the release of slaves in order to avoid the concentration of wealth in the hands of a few and the development of a perpetual underclass. In addition, there was the year of Jubilee, in which all land that had been sold was returned to its original families, again to avoid the concentration of wealth and production in the hands of a few, insuring whole family systems were not doomed to servitude throughout generations.

One of my favorite guiding principles involves the tithes which were brought into the temple. Every third year, the tithes which were paid were to be distributed among the poor, the widows, the fatherless and the aliens.

> *When you have finished setting aside a tenth of all your produce in the third year, the year of the tithe,* **you shall give it to the Levite, the alien, the fatherless and the widow, so that they may eat in your towns and be satisfied.** *Then say to the LORD your God: "I have removed from my house the sacred portion and have given it to the Levite, the alien, the fatherless and the widow, according to all you commanded. Deut. 26:12ff*

The overall impression you get is that God intended that everyone who lived within His Kingdom would have equal opportunity for success and have all their necessities met. He goes so far as to state that if these decrees were fully followed, poverty would not exist in their society.

God directed that these guidelines and commandments, these laws, were to be diligently taught from generation to generation. Not only were they to be the focus of formal instruction, they were also to be informally passed on by parents to their children during normal everyday activities. Daily obedience and modeling by the parents to the children would ensure that God would continue to bless Israel and act as its defender. As we saw earlier in Deuteronomy 11:18-22, the Israelites were responsible for teaching their children about God and His plans for humankind. God was calling them to authentically live for Him. He challenged them to use symbols such as putting the word on the doorposts of the house as reminders and binding the word of God as jewelry to their bodies. His intent was that life would be permeated with the knowledge of Him.

In spite of God's mercy and kindness in leading His people out of slavery in Egypt, of demonstrations of His goodness through providing their daily needs, of protecting them from enemies more powerful than them, of leading them into the land filled with milk and honey and fulfilling all His promises to them, there was still a great mistrust of God and His intentions. He was viewed with suspicion. From the time of the Israelites liberation from Egypt, throughout their journey in the wilderness, an undercurrent of rebellion and hostility poisoned the people's interactions with God.

Within a few years, recorded in I Samuel 8, this underlying fear and suspicion of God is given a voice as the people explain how they would like to live apart from God's rule. God warns the people that their choice comes with a hefty price to their liberty, their economic well-being and family security. Nevertheless, the people choose, and in a way, their choice acts as an archetype of how people and societies would choose to live their lives throughout the remainder of history.

*...But when they said, **"Give us a king to lead us,"** this displeased Samuel; so he prayed to the LORD. 1Sam. 8:4*

*And the LORD told him: "Listen to all that the people are saying to you; it is not you they have rejected, but they have rejected me as their king. As they have done from the day I brought them up out of Egypt until this day, forsaking me and serving other gods, so they are doing to you. Now listen to them; **but warn them solemnly and let them know what the king who will reign over them will claim as his rights."** 1Sam. 8:7*

*But the people refused to listen to Samuel. "No!" they said. **"We want a king over us. Then we will be like all the other nations, with a king to lead us and to go out before us and fight our battles."** 1Sam. 8:19 (emphasis mine)*

We want our own way. We are suspicious of God, the King of Kings. We are fearful. In our desire to throw off any standard of God's, we create for ourselves a pattern of living based upon that of people around us who do not know God. We gain a sense of security through conforming to cultural patterns. This sense of security through conformity eventually is expressed through traditions. Tribal associations (in-group or out-group distinctions such as associating ourselves with ethnicities, racial groups, classes of people, cultural fads or sub-cultural groups), intellectual or political ideologies, and religious systems are created that take the place of God in our life. We even conform while shouting vocally or through our lifestyle that we are non-conformists. Sometimes the conformity is good, sending us in directions that are helpful, healthful and uplifting. More often the conformity is bad, causing us to compromise our sense of self or deeply held values and raising doubts within us regarding our way of life or life direction. Whatever the expression, if it demands an allegiance to someone or something other than God, it is an expression of rebellion. As such, it leaves us knowing that there must be more. Our culture, clan, or clique can't meet the deeply ingrained need God placed within us for a relationship with Him. Tragically, we know no other way to live, so we fight against ideas contrary to ours, clinging to a deeply flawed lifestyle because it is the only one we know, and the only one with which we are comfortable.

Jesus encountered the power of conformity through tradition, culture and clan when he initiated His ministry.

He went to Nazareth, where he had been brought up, and on the Sabbath day he went into the synagogue, as was his custom. He stood up to read, and the scroll of the prophet Isaiah was handed to him. Unrolling it, he found the place where it is written:

"The Spirit of the Lord is on me, because he has anointed me to proclaim good news to the poor. He has sent me to proclaim freedom for the prisoners and recovery of sight for the blind, to set the oppressed free, to proclaim the year of the Lord's favor."

Then he rolled up the scroll, gave it back to the attendant and sat down. The eyes of everyone in the synagogue were fastened on him. He began by saying to them, **"Today this scripture is fulfilled in your hearing."**

All spoke well of him *and were amazed at the gracious words that came from his lips. "Isn't this Joseph's son?" they asked. Luke 4:16ff*

*Jesus said to them, "Surely you will quote this proverb to me: 'Physician, heal yourself!' And you will tell me, 'Do here in your hometown what we have heard that you did in Capernaum.' " "Truly I tell you," he continued, "prophets are not accepted in their home- towns. I assure you that there were many widows in Israel in Elijah's time, when the sky was shut for three and a half years and there was a severe famine throughout the land. **Yet Elijah was not sent to any of them, but to a widow in Zarephath in the region of Sidon.** And there were many in Israel with leprosy in the time of Elisha the prophet, yet not one of them was cleansed—only Naaman the Syrian." Luke 4:23*

All the people in the synagogue were furious when they heard this. They got up, drove him out of the town, and took him to the brow of the hill on which the town was built, in order to throw him off the cliff. *But he walked right through the crowd and went on his way. Luke 4:28 (emphasis mine)*

Note the bold sections. When Jesus read from the portion of Isaiah on the Kingdom of God, the people were ecstatic because the culturally prevalent interpretation was that this would benefit solely the Jews and be disastrous for all gen- tiles. It fit in well with the tribal manner in which Israel had come to understand God and His promises. Jesus turns this cultural understanding on its head by taking an example from Elijah, a prophet from Galilee, where he was currently speaking, and pointing out that God chose a gentile widow in a gentile land to protect Elijah rather than a Jewish widow in Israel. The result is an infuriated crowd that wants to kill Jesus for His embracing of the gentiles (a dominant theme throughout Kingdom passages). Jesus radically adheres to what the scriptures teach about the Kingdom and the religious and political powers couldn't stand the message. Teaching about God and His intentions tends to be palatable to us if it confirms our biases, prejudices and cultural patterns. When it doesn't we resist it to the point of denying its very existence or truthfulness. The apostle Paul explained it as follows in Romans 1:18-19:

> *The wrath of God is being revealed from heaven against all the godlessness and wickedness of human beings **who suppress the truth by their wickedness**, since what may be known about God is plain to them, because God has made it plain to them. (emphasis mine)*

God's truth is suppressed, held down, or hidden, not by ideology or philosophy so much as whether or not it is compatible with how people want to live their lives (wickedness after all is not heinous action, it's merely living apart from God and His will). So, in place of God and His Kingdom, humans erect their own kingdoms, socially and personally, and invent their own things to worship.

These kingdoms are in conflict with God and His Kingdom. The resolution of this conflict points to one person, Jesus, and one point in time, His death, burial and resurrection. Jesus reveals God's character to us. He holds the full teaching of the Kingdom in Himself. He Himself is the door to the Kingdom. His sacrifice for our sin breaks down the hostility between us and God, and between other people. His resurrection affirms the worthiness and God's acceptance of His sacrifice and assures us that He has the power to accomplish what He came into the world to accomplish.

> *The one who does what is sinful is of the devil, because the devil has been sinning from the begin-*

*ning. **The reason the Son of God appeared was to
destroy the devil's work.** 1Jn. 3:8 (emphasis mine)*

Destroying the work of the devil was the focus of Jesus'
ministry and it becomes the focus of ours as we seek to
follow Him. Ultimately, the victory over the devil was won
with the crucifixion, burial and resurrection of Jesus.

*... **And having disarmed the powers and authorities,
he made a public spectacle of them, triumphing
over them by the cross.** Col. 2:13 (emphasis mine)*

Practically, the work on earth of destroying the work of
the devil needs to be completed by us, His followers, who are
now referred to as the "body of Christ". We are His hands
and feet in the world. We are His voice. We embody His
values and demonstrate to the world what God is like, why
He can be entrusted with our lives and future, and why following Him is not only sensible, but fulfilling.

So...God's character and will are revealed in His
Kingdom. God's intentions for humankind are revealed in
the Kingdom. The Kingdom is rooted in the character of
God. Therefore, **to reject Kingdom principles or what the
Kingdom teaches about what His followers are to be like
is to reject God** (Matt. 12:30). You cannot break the King's
law and not have Him take it personally. Our assumptions
about God and our willingness to submit to Him determine
our receptivity to the Kingdom. The next chapter takes a look
at the demands of the Kingdom of God upon His followers.

Summary
We find ourselves as central players in an amazing
drama in which God is working out a plan throughout history which not only remedies the damage done by sin within
individuals, but the damage done in creation and society.

Through the death, burial and resurrection of His Son, Jesus, God provides redemption from sin and its effects for those who choose to follow Jesus and accept His forgiving work. Those who follow Jesus are to be involved in the work Jesus launched, destruction of the works of the devil. Jesus' followers are His hands, feet and voice in the world. We as His followers have been given the task of reconciling people to God and bringing about reconciliation in society.

God has revealed for us His grand plan in the scriptures and it is referred to as the Kingdom of God. Within its teachings are principles which define for us how God would like us to live in the world and how He would envision our societies to function.

We as His followers are to embody these principles and live lives that are windows into the heart of God. Our trust in God and the positive effects it manifests in our lives serves to disarm resistance others may have in living lives in obedience to God.

There is no neutral ground in this grand story. **You either align yourself with God or you stand in opposition against Him. To do nothing is to choose rebellion.**

*After our return from our summer mission trip in West Virginia, our church, Soncoast, started up a "**Mission As Life**" Wednesday night service that Addie....... Has been heading up, and it's been such a blessing in so many ways to know the needs in our community and to jump in and help!* **We made bags filled with non-perishable foods to keep in our cars for when we come across hungry people on the street, we will have something to give them! We put tracts and notes in the bags too. The little kids made some trail mix in their youth meeting and put little bags of the trail mix in each of the bags too. Everyone felt good that we were going to be helping people!!!!** *Connie FL*

Chapter 4

Discovering what God expects of your family

When I was going through premarital counseling years ago, the counselor asked me a question that eventually had me on the verge of a panic (it felt like it at the time). It was a simple question, *How do you know you really love this young lady and that this is not just a passing infatuation?* He shot down all my initial responses such as, "I can't stop thinking about her." (A mere sign of infatuation.) Eventually I realized that my love for her was manifest in my levels of commitment, my willingness to sacrifice, serve, and work for her best interests. Love is commitment, and emotion is sometimes a thermometer for that commitment. As fickle as emotions can be, commitment is more stable and is able to drag emotions to where they should be.

I found that my relationship with the Kingdom of God has led me through the same process of emotional attraction and deep commitment I found in my love for my beautiful wife. My wife is the focus of my passion physically and emotionally in terms of human relationships. **What is my passion in terms of how I live in the world?**

What is your passion?

The world certainly has a smorgasbord of passions from which we may choose. Advertising and marketing exist to quicken passions in us we never knew we needed or even wanted, or never knew existed. As you sit back and examine the world and all its messages, themes, and demands, what would you say are the passions it promotes?

Take a minute and ask yourself this question. What is my passion? What do you find yourself thinking about in those moments when an immediate task is not demanding your attention? When you have large blocks of "free time", how do you desire to spend it? If an independent observer were to come in and examine your life over the period of a month, what would they determine your life theme to be? Would what you profess to be your dominant values and goals be verified by how you spend your time, your treasures and your talents?

God has a claim on your life. If you are a follower of Jesus, God has absolute right to every aspect of your life because He purchased it (redeemed it) outright by the sacrifice of His Son for your sins (Romans 6 beautifully describes this). Consequently, we have no right to our lives, once we come to follow Jesus. We live at the pleasure of the King, and should also serve according to His pleasure.

When I was first born again, I remember an old deacon telling me, *Just because kittens are born in an oven, it doesn't make them biscuits.* Just because you attend church and have since you were little, it doesn't make you a follower of Jesus. Those who follow Jesus have had a personal encounter with Him. Look at the language used in scripture to show the effect of that relationship.

*"The kingdom of heaven is like treasure hidden in a field. When a man found it, he hid it again, and then **in his joy went and sold all he had and bought***

that field. *"Again, the kingdom of heaven is like a merchant looking for fine pearls.* **When he found one of great value, he went away and sold everything he had and bought it.***" Matt. 13:44 (emphasis mine)*

When you truly encounter Jesus, when you truly come face to face with the reality that God is just in punishing you for your myriad of sins (no matter how seemingly trivial), when you realize that any chance of forgiveness is purely traceable to the grace of God, when you fully grasp the suffering and love Jesus displayed on the cross to bring about your forgiveness, your response cannot be anything less than what is explained in the above passages. Wholehearted devotion and obedience to Christ is the logical and only response to so great a sacrifice. The idea that you can somehow embrace the salvation of Jesus and avoid hell (fire insurance), without loving and following Him completely is foreign to scripture and borders on heresy. There may be deathbed conversions as evidenced by the thief on the cross, but for the most part it involves a relinquishing of sovereignty of our lives to God. Does that mean we cease to sin or are perfect? Not at all! It means we repent of our sin and lifestyle and yield our lives and futures to the Lord.

> *Let the wicked forsake their ways and the unrighteous their thoughts. Let them turn to the LORD, and he will have mercy on them, and to our God, for he will freely pardon. For my thoughts are not your thoughts, neither are your ways my ways,"* *declares the LORD. As the heavens are higher than the earth, so are my ways higher than your ways and my thoughts than your thoughts. Isa. 55:7*

The word "thoughts" can best be translated "thoughts, plans and ambitions". God's thoughts, plans and ambitions are not the same as ours. We abandon ours to embrace His! This makes sense when we look at what Jesus taught...

> But **seek first His kingdom and His righteousness**, *and all these things will be given to you as well. Therefore do not worry about tomorrow, for tomorrow will worry about itself. Each day has enough trouble of its own. Matt. 6:33 (emphasis mine)*

Seeking first God's Kingdom means we must abandon our thoughts, plans and ambitions for our future and embrace God's vision for the future. Does that mean we become a bunch of professional religionists? God forbid!! What it means is that the trajectory of our lives is not determined by any personal, cultural, social, economic, or political vision. It is to be determined by God who has redeemed us and placed within us the potential for greatness when we submit our gifts and abilities to advancing His Kingdom. The special interests, the gifts, the abilities, the talents we have received from God begin to blossom when we allow Him to direct our paths in life.

We can never achieve our full potential until we align ourselves with God's purposes. When we do, not only do we benefit, all creation benefits, all society benefits, our families benefit. Barren places are made fruitful. The destructive is replaced with the enriching. Cynicism and sadness are replaced with hope and joy.

When we follow the passions of the world, we imperil our very souls. When we adapt as our pattern for living the patterns of those who seem prosperous in society, we squander our personal value on tawdry trinkets. The short-term, superficial fulfillment embraced by our society seems so alluring and fulfilling. However, as followers of Jesus, we must forgo those siren songs and instead lose our lives, by current standards, and pursue God and His Kingdom. When we do, we find an exhilarating reality. Losing our lives; abandoning our "thoughts, plans and ambitions" and embracing God's "thoughts, plans and ambitions", opens us up to discovering our true selves.

> *Then he said to them all: "Whoever wants to be my disciple must deny themselves and take up their cross daily and follow me. **For whoever wants to save their life will lose it, but whoever loses their life for me will save it**. What good is it for you to gain the whole world, and yet lose or forfeit your very self?" Luke 9:23*

Continuing in our own direction, following our own thoughts and ambitions, living as if God doesn't exist, impoverishes our soul, reducing us to caricatures of full human beings. We become personas, rather than persons. We live scripts in our life that are like quick takes in a movie, sitcoms of false, plastic people. The world becomes merely a stage and our parts the hollow shells of real life.

"Follow me" means...

The language Jesus uses is appropriate. We must deny ourselves, put to death those ideas, ambitions, or worldviews that are so intoxicating and attractive, and that ultimately stand as alternatives to following God and doing His will. This is what is meant by taking up your cross daily and following Him. It is serious and strikes at the heart of all the world has to offer.

> *As they were walking along the road, a man said to him, "I will follow you wherever you go." Jesus replied, **"Foxes have holes and birds have nests, but***

*the Son of Man has no place to lay his head." Luke
9:57 (emphasis mine)*

The response to Jesus seems so sincere. Yet, Jesus strikes
to the heart, "Are you willing to be homeless?" or, "Are you
willing to give up the American Dream?" For Jesus, it's
always an allegiance thing. He wants all of us, not part of
us. He makes it clear that ambition apart from God is ambition directed against God and His divine intentions. It points
back to the very temptation that destroyed Adam and Eve
and put us in this awful predicament today. It stresses that
aligning oneself with God may be costly. It may seem illog-
ical in terms of current fashion and wisdom. It may place
you in precarious circumstances and situations in which you
are thrown onto trusting God for your very existence.

*He said to another man, "Follow me." But he replied,
"Lord, first let me go and bury my father." Jesus said
to him, "Let the dead bury their own dead, but you
go and proclaim the kingdom of God." Luke 9:59
(emphasis mine)*

Again, the one seeking Jesus seems so sincere. Again
Jesus poses a question which cuts like a knife, exposing
allegiances. Jesus wants to find out if any cultural or social
expectation will take precedence over obeying and following
Him. The burial of a father was and is a powerful cultural
expectation. What made it even more powerful is the reality
that the one asked to forego the burial may have been the
one to whom the father's inheritance would be assigned.
Would you be willing to face cultural censure and gossip
because of your absence as well as the possible loss of some
inheritance?

*Still another said, "I will follow you, Lord; but first let me go back and say good-by to my family." Jesus replied, **"No one who puts a hand to the plow and looks back is fit for service in the kingdom of God."** Luke 9:61 (emphasis mine)*

Followers must have no demands pulling them back into their old life. They must have no regrets about launching out with God. However comfy, exciting, interesting, personally gratifying the old life, the follower's eye is focused on where God is taking him or her, not what he or she has done or left behind. As Paul stated, they must count all those things as "dung", to be cast off and forgotten.

What Jesus is addressing in these passages relates to what later was listed as one of the seven deadly sins, sloth. Interestingly enough, sloth is not mere laziness. What it originally referred to was spiritual indifference which was often evidenced in involvement in activities which drew one away from primary responsibilities to love and serve God. You can be busy doing many important and good activities, but according to Luke 9, find yourself torn in whether or not to obey God in doing what He has commanded. Jesus makes it clear that there is to be a disengagement from the kind of thinking which places personal comfort or safety, familial or cultural obligations, and nostalgic or romantic notions regarding the past ahead of following God. He makes it clear that the work to which He calls us demands our full attention and requires dying to many of the accepted values and agendas of our culture.

The idea of dying to various aspects of life tends to get a lopsided presentation in most of our churches. The idea that we must die to clearly sinful or destructive acts, alcoholism, drug addiction, sexual promiscuity, greed or thievery is talked about regularly. However, the need to die to activities which are good, uplifting and wholesome gets little attention. These are more difficult to rationalize. Their potential for mischief lies in their ability to draw our attention from God and His will, to "good activity". The very goodness of some actions becomes sinful when it is a substitute for the will of God in our lives. These very activities produce a poverty of time and resources. They eat up time we could spend in service to God or in fellowship with Him. I believe this over-commitment to good activities is one of the most prevalent sins today. When these potential idols are targeted by God, they can stir up trouble that makes us wonder if we are doing the right thing. Jesus knew of this and spoke directly to it.

> *"I have come to bring fire on the earth, and how I wish it were already kindled! But I have a baptism to undergo, and what constraint I am under until it is completed! Do you think I came to bring peace on earth? No, I tell you, but division." Luke 12:49 ff (emphasis mine)*

Our need for a peaceful, stable life can be a barrier to following God. Our desire to make the best of every opportunity, commit our children to myriads of activities for their "enrichment" and tie up all of our resources in developing "personal worth" ends up diluting our commitment to the Lord. When approached about deeper commitment and service to Christ we state we are over-committed already. But over-committed to what? Are these things Kingdom related? And, when I say Kingdom related, I don't necessarily mean church related either. Churches can over commit people to activities which can often be explained as religious "self-help" activities which are just as damaging as counter to Kingdom values as deciding to take a class on ballroom dancing. The activities aren't evil, they are merely dissipating. Love of church and church activities can become idolatrous. (What does God say true religion involves? James 1:27) The King demands complete allegiance, allowing no rival for our heart. He is jealous and will not play second fiddle to any person, position, desire or ambition. The completeness of this allegiance is explained in stark terminology.

*Large crowds were traveling with Jesus, and turning to them he said: **"If anyone comes to me and does not hate father and mother, wife and children, brothers and sisters—yes, even life itself—such a person cannot be my disciple.** And whoever does not carry their cross and follow me cannot be my disciple". Luke 14:25*

In the same way, those of you who do not give up everything you have cannot be my disciples. *"Salt is good, but if it loses its saltiness, how can it be made salty again? It is fit neither for the soil nor for the manure pile; it is thrown out. "Whoever has ears to hear, let them hear." Luke 14:33 (emphasis mine)*

Everyone in our family knew that it was expected that our ultimate allegiance would be to Jesus. That meant that the direction of our lives, the relationships we had with one another, the safety of one another, all our resources, were secondary to doing the will of God and serving Him. The love and devotion we have toward God should make all other relationships or affiliations seem as though they were worth nothing. We willingly limited our involvement in various activities in order to free up time for not only service, but reflection and solitude with the Lord.

I believe one of the most difficult principles for people to grasp is that doing good things can actually be sinful. When sin is defined as anything which opposes the will of God, it becomes easier to grasp the concept. **Just because you can**

do something doesn't mean you should. The ability to say no to things that are "good" in order to concentrate on those things which are "best" requires discipline and a heart tuned to the voice of the Spirit of God. Enforcing this type of discipline can lead to conflict as family members individually deal with their own self-centeredness.

Does this mean God seeks to break up families, put us through misery, deny us any pleasure or foster strife in our lives? By all means no. He came that He might give us a life that is full and deliver us from the emptiness of selfish indulgence or the blind duty of tradition, cultural demands and social convention. In fact, placing allegiance to Christ at the center of all our family's relationships, all our plans and all our ambitions catapulted our lives into a higher level of satisfaction and fulfillment. Our lives became more full, our relationships were deeper, our ambitions more challenging and humane. Placing Christ at the center of our lives so enriched us that we seemed at times to feel as though we would almost burst with joy.

The thief comes only to steal and kill and destroy; **I have come that they may have life, and have it to the full.** *Jn. 10:10 (emphasis mine)*

This passage stands as a declaration that a truly fulfilling life is wrapped up in life with God. Jesus seeks people who are totally abandoned to Him. They should have a love so strong that it severs the strongest ties on earth. He wants us to be sold out to Him. Nothing will be accepted as an excuse for not making Him and His Kingdom your obsession. God wants our love; we are to love Him supremely. How do we know if we love Him?

Obedience is not a four letter word

Obedience is almost considered a dirty word in some churches, yet it exists as a foundational, identifying characteristic of those who follow Jesus. Failing to obey Him may expose us as false followers, only inquisitive seekers who were testing the waters, having a divided allegiance.

"If you love me, keep my commands". Jn. 14:15

*Jesus replied, "**Anyone who loves me will obey my teaching.** My Father will love them, and we will come to them and make our home with them. Anyone who does not love me will not obey my teaching. These words you hear are not my own; they belong to the Father who sent me." Jn. 14:23*

***If you keep my commands, you will remain in my love, just as I have kept my Father's commands and remain in his love.** Jn. 15:10*

***We know that we have come to know him if we keep his commands.** Those who say, "I know Him," but do not do what he commands are liars, and the truth is not in them. But if anyone obeys his word, love for God is truly made complete in them. I Jn. 2:3 (emphasis mine)*

Obedience to what He has taught reveals the genuineness of our love.

***If any one of you has material possessions and sees a brother or sister in need but has no pity on them, how can the love of God be in you?** Dear children, let us not love with words or tongue but with actions and in truth. 1 Jn. 3:15*

*We love because he first loved us. If we say we love God yet hate a brother or sister, we are liars. **For if we do not love a fellow believer, whom we have seen, we cannot love God, whom we have not seen.** And he has given us this command: Those who love God must also love one another. 1 Jn. 4:19*

*And this is love: that we **walk in obedience** to his commands. As you have heard from the beginning, his command is that you walk in love. 2 Jn. 1:6 (emphasis mine)*

The Kingdom of God demands we obey the King. The Lord calls to us with His first and most important call. The LORD says, come to Me, love Me supremely, have fellowship with Me. Turning to Him requires turning from something else (repenting need not be entirely related to sin, it is deeper than that). The lie of the evil one is that when we turn to God, we somehow diminish ourselves, deprive ourselves of what is "the highest good", and squander our futures. The reality is that when we turn to God we open doors of opportunity forever closed otherwise. We open ourselves to the life of the Eternal One, the One who can take the embryonic potentials of our giftedness, our talents, and our resources and grow them to birth a life jam-packed with meaning, wonder, significance, and hope. He enables us to fully grasp "reality" and bridge the gap between eternity and everyday life. He enables us to tap into the power behind the universe and see how it transforms first ourselves, and then the world around us. Here are some examples of some who left all to follow Jesus.

When he had finished speaking, he said to Simon, "Put out into deep water, and let down the nets for a catch."

101

Simon answered, "Master, we've worked hard all night and haven't caught anything. But because you say so, I will let down the nets."

When they had done so, they caught such a large number of fish that their nets began to break. So they signaled their partners in the other boat to come and help them, and they came and filled both boats so full that they began to sink. When Simon Peter saw this, he fell at Jesus' knees and said, "Go away from me, Lord; I am a sinful man!"

*For he and all his companions were astonished at the catch of fish they had taken, and so were James and John, the sons of Zebedee, Simon's partners. **Then Jesus said to Simon, "Don't be afraid; from now on you will fish for people."***

***So they pulled their boats up on shore, left everything and followed him.** Luke 5:4-11*

What a story. The Zebedee and Sons Fishery have one of the biggest catches of its history. It "sets the market" with its catch and ensures high profits and a new influx of capital. In the midst of this success, the call comes to leave it all behind and follow Jesus. The miracle in this story is not the draught of fish, it is that Simon and the Zebedee brothers leave all and follow Jesus. Their hearts were put in awe of Jesus; they felt they found a treasure greater than the one they had just harvested.

*After this, Jesus went out and saw a tax collector by the name of Levi sitting at his tax booth. **"Follow me," Jesus said to him, and Levi got up, left everything and followed him.** Luke 5:27 (emphasis mine)*

Another miracle! Here on the seamy side of life, Jesus calls another successful businessman, one whose future is set for life if he plays his cards right. Still, Levi leaves it all behind to follow. He steps from what appears to be certain security into what appears to be certain insecurity.

Jesus entered Jericho and was passing through. A man was there by the name of Zacchaeus; he was a chief tax collector and was wealthy. He wanted to see who Jesus was, but because he was short he could not see over the crowd. So he ran ahead and climbed a sycamore-fig tree to see him, since Jesus was coming that way.

When Jesus reached the spot, he looked up and said to him, "Zacchaeus, come down immediately. I must stay at your house today."

So he came down at once and welcomed him gladly.

...But Zacchaeus stood up and said to the Lord, "Look, Lord! Here and now I give half of my posses- sions to the poor, and if I have cheated anybody out of anything, I will pay back four times the amount."
Luke 19:1-8

What's up with the tax collectors? In this instance, Jesus so captures the heart of Zacchaeus that he vows to make restitution to all those whom he has cheated and then give half of all he owns to the poor. Now that's a miracle!

In each of these instances, you have people whose hearts have been captured by Christ. When they act, they act out of passionate love. What once was their passion, making money, was replaced by a passion for God.

In each instance, people left what appeared to be a "secure" or "safe" situation or career, and embarked on a journey in which security and safety seemed to evaporate. Let me tell you, there is no security or safety apart from the will of God. It's an illusion. Recent developments in our financial markets have shown the hollowness of putting one's trust in riches. The scripture is full of stories which prove this, one of the best being one I call Bigger Barns.

> ... *"The ground of a certain rich man yielded an abundant harvest. He thought to himself, 'What shall I do? I have no place to store my crops.' "Then he said, 'This is what I'll do. I will tear down my barns and build bigger ones, and there I will store my surplus grain. And I'll say to myself,* **"You have plenty of grain laid up for many years. Take life easy; eat, drink and be merry."** *' But God said to him, 'You fool! This very night your life will be demanded from you. Then who will get what you have prepared for yourself?'* **"This is how it will be with those who store up things for themselves but are not rich toward God."** *Luke 12:16-20 (emphasis mine)*

I think Bigger Barns is the parable of the American lifestyle. Mr. Barns thought that his windfall was for his own use, his security, his retirement. He had forgotten that **God blesses us in order that we would be a blessing to others.** He forgot that security resides in following God, not in the abundance of money or power. Mr. Barns was suffering from slothfulness, indifference to the things of God. Consequently, God decided it was time for him to check out. I have often wondered if the rich man mentioned in Luke 16:19, was the same person.

What should be our response to the Kingdom of God?

It's clear that our response to the Kingdom is dependent upon the condition of our hearts, where our true affections lie. What we must do is guard our hearts from dissipation, from conflicting allegiances, from activities which consume our time, our treasure and our talents. We must be careful to nurture our love for Jesus. We must set aside the time to study the word of God and pray. We must set aside the time to put what we have studied into action in our families and in our communities. We must move from an information orientation to an action orientation. Having our primary goal of following God to be the acquisition of knowledge reduces it to mere religious intellectualism. Allowing ourselves to become busy with all kinds of service, and neglecting God's word, prayer and fellowship with the Lord, makes us mere social activists. What is required is balance. **We must learn the will of God and do it.** We must take our flickering light of faith and renew it daily in the blazing light of God's Son. To offer life to the world, we must daily partake of the bread of life. We cannot minister life out of death. We must be vitally connected to the resurrection life in God's Son, Jesus. We cannot "bottle up" that life connection turning it into something that exists only for our emotional benefit. We must release that life daily, allowing it to flow through us to an injured and hungry world.

Being and doing are often juxtaposed, contrasted in sermons and in writing. To be truly healthy, we must join them together daily. There is a time for prayer and a time for work. However, I like what Mother Teresa said, *Pray the work.* Blend the being and doing together into a seamless activity. Our study and fellowship with God informs us of His will and nurtures our understanding of Him and His character increasing our ability to trust Him. Our service softens our hearts, breaks down barriers in our lives and more importantly, proves what we have studied to be true. Our service reveals God to be trustworthy, faithful, dependable and truly out for our best interests.

Most importantly, God calls us to a life with Him. The Kingdom of God presupposes a relationship with God. It is not about politics or living out some script in your daily life. It's being passionate about God. It's loving Jesus because of His great sacrifice. Our relationship to the Kingdom of God is really our relationship to the King, God Himself. Having our heart captured by Him, being passionate in our love for Him and allowing this passion to be lived out in our daily life makes the Kingdom of God visible to those around us.

It is interesting that in the auditing verses (those verses you find in scripture where God has called a group before Him for judgment), a recurring theme arises. Ultimately, God judges us on whether or not He "knows" us.

> *Then I will tell them plainly, '**I never knew you.** Away from me, you evildoers!' Matt. 7:23 (emphasis mine)*

When we develop a relationship with Christ that goes beyond formality, that becomes a personal love affair with God, we begin to assimilate God's sense of priority in the world and embrace His heart. We begin to see how God would like us to live in the world, how our lives can begin to live out His intentions for humankind and how we can make a unique contribution to advancing His Kingdom, ultimately making the world a better place.

Summary

Do you love Him? Has He captured your heart? Here is the crux of following God. Loving Him is manifest in how much you obey Him, how much you put into practice what He commanded regarding how we are to live in the world.

Loving Him requires making choices, choices which involve selecting the highest good and consequently, making other things appear to be somewhat cheap and unworthy of our attention. Those around us will misunderstand; they may be hurt or become angry. They may feel rejected. We may feel as though we have become traitorous to our culture or our family. Our affections will be strained as our allegiance is tested. An evil one waits to burden us with a false shame, accusations, and a yoke of ostracism. Every possible emotional tie, every mental ambition, every cultural expectation will be brought to bear to get us to do one thing, disobey.

One day we will stand before Him and give an account of all we have said and done. His first question will probably be, "Did you love me?" We really don't want to be in the position where in shame we hang our heads and say, *Oh Lord, we should have loved you more*.

I served with Mustard Seeds and Mountains on a spring break trip from college. I was a sophomore. It was my first mission trip and awoke my heart to the needs of the poor, even the poor that were in my own country! I had no idea such poverty existed outside of the inner city. Anyway, I remember Randy's talk on the Kingdom of God, and also a little about God's heart for the poor throughout Scripture. Those two things still stick with me, and I remember thinking, "How could I have gone to a Christian college and never heard about how much God loves the poor? Why doesn't anyone talk about this?"

Our church is just starting the curriculum Compassion by Command, written by Here's Life Inner City. I am hoping it will awaken more hearts to the needy in our community, and how to reach them with compassion. Linnea, MN

Chapter 5

Making God's priorities your family's priorities

M any of the songs we sing in worship talk of our desire to be close to God. We pray for Him to come down in power, to reveal Himself to us, to embrace us, to move in and change the world. Some of us become more intimate and cry out for a deep knowing of Him to the point where our hearts are brought in tune with His heart, a melding of our life and purpose with that of God's. This level of intimacy is the highest level we can achieve in our finite lives. I liken it to placing your head on the bosom of God and hearing Him talk to Himself in a soft whisper, a sigh of yearning as He reveals what is on His heart. Isaiah experienced this.

In Isaiah 6 he gives his account of how drawing near to God in His unfathomable holiness and magnitude struck Isaiah down as a dead man and peeled back his veneer of respectability to expose his sin. You can hear Isaiah's awe and his terror as he confesses his sin and identifies with the sins of his community, his province and his nation.

When God cleanses Isaiah of his sin, Isaiah draws near enough to God to hear Him reveal His passion. The wave of

God's love and His pain flows over Isaiah as he hears Him ask *"…whom can we send and who will go for us?"* **Isaiah in that moment is exposed to the totality of God's character and plans.** Within that statement reside all the seeds of reconciliation, redemption, grace, justice, atonement, that resound throughout the scriptures, echo in eternity, and are captured in numerous stories of God. It is seeking those who have abandoned Him and live as if He doesn't exist, injuring themselves in countless ways and squandering His good gifts lavished upon them.

This chapter is about the heart of God and what He has declared to be important. It isolates the priorities of God. It doesn't cover them all; it provides an overview of the dominant themes in Scripture regarding God's purposes. All are action-oriented versus theoretical orientations.

Conformity's danger and the need to go against the cultural grain

We have all been trained to conform to those around us. It began when our mothers first dressed us and was accelerated in earnest when we entered the school system. Most of us grew up looking at what people were doing around us and correcting or modifying our behavior, beliefs or goals based upon what we discovered. We each selected our own particular group to be our reference standard. Since we tend to congregate with people like us, we soon begin to think that only the behaviors, values and ambitions of our group are "right" and "normal". Appearances, activities and aspirations not consistent with our referent group are seen as suspect or downright wrong and to be avoided. The sense of group solidarity which has been socialized into us serves as the guiding light in most people's lives. What is good or bad is determined by what those around us are doing, what those in our in group model.

This tendency is not only dangerous, it embraces the very root of the first sin, the one Adam and Eve were enticed to commit. It fosters that same sense of mistrust, suspicion and rejection of God that infected Adam and Eve. The Apostle Paul refers to this error in the following way…

*We do not dare to classify or compare ourselves with some who commend themselves. When they measure themselves by themselves and compare themselves with themselves, **they are not wise**. 2Cor. 10:12 (emphasis mine)*

"Evil associations corrupt good works." In other words, friends who are good, respectable, kind, and responsible, but who live as though God doesn't exist, can corrupt our lives and put us in opposition to God and His plans. This is just as dangerous and sinful as hanging with friends who are involved in illegal activity. It is essential that we unshackle our minds from the tyranny of conformity. We must transform ourselves by the renewing of our mind. We must become immersed in God's perspective on how to live and work in the world.

One of the most well-known declarations of God's perspective on how people should live in the world is found in Micah 6:8.

*He has shown all you people what is good. And what does the LORD require of you? To **act justly** and to **love mercy** and to **walk humbly** with your God. Mic. 6:8 (emphasis mine)*

Acting justly, loving mercy, walking humbly, these themes resound throughout scripture. They reflect the very nature of God as revealed in Christ Jesus. Isaiah speaks of Jesus as the servant of God in Isaiah 42.

*"Here is my servant, whom I uphold, my chosen one in whom I delight; I will put my Spirit on him, and **he will bring justice to the nations**. Isa. 42:1*

He will not shout or cry out, or raise his voice in the streets. *A bruised reed he will not break, and a smoldering wick he will not snuff out. In faithfulness he will bring forth justice; he will not falter or be discouraged till he establishes justice on earth. In his teaching the islands will put their hope." Isa. 42:2 (emphasis mine)*

It is this tenderness, the unwillingness to snuff out any glimmer of light in a person's life, the unwillingness to act in a manner that causes those bent under the weight of their own poor choices to break under added strain that reflects the life and character of God. As we serve Him in reaching out to others, we must recognize any glimmer of hope, any sign of previous work in their lives by God. No matter how badly the image of God is damaged in them currently, we use gentleness and kindness to nurture them back to strength and fan the flame of their light.

*... "I, the LORD, have called you in righteousness; I will take hold of your hand. I will keep you and will make you to be a covenant for the people and a light for the Gentiles, **to open eyes that are blind, to free captives from prison and to release from the dungeon those who sit in darkness**." Isa. 42:5 (emphasis mine)*

As the passage points out, justice involves releasing people who are blind, captive, and lost in the dark from the things which oppress and enslave them. **Justice is the work and calling of all who follow God.** It doesn't reside in the court systems of the world. It is anchored in our daily lives and how we treat others and allow them to be treated. We are called to operationally act out justice in our daily lives and in our communities.

> *"This is what the LORD Almighty said: '**Administer true justice; show mercy and compassion to one another. Do not oppress the widow or the fatherless, the foreigner or the poor. Do not plot evil against each other.'** Zech. 7:9 (emphasis mine)*

Some say, "Wait, those are verses in the Old Testament. Do they apply to us in the church?" The best answer is to look at the Sermon on the Mount in Matthew.

> *Blessed are those who **hunger and thirst for righteousness** for they will be filled. Matt. 5:6 (emphasis mine)*

The word translated "righteousness" or "righteous" in the New Testament is most often the word translated justice in the Old Testament passages. God's heart beats a cadence of a quest for justice for all those who follow Him. He expects our hearts to synchronize with His. Why? Because if we love God, we will love those made in His image.

> *Anyone who says he loves God but in fact hates his brother or sister is a liar. He doesn't love his brother or sister, whom he has seen. So he can't love God, whom he has not seen. I John 4:20.*

At the heart of our life as Christians should be a desire to see justice done throughout the world. Whenever we see it in short supply we should suffer as we would suffer physically for food and water. It is that vital to us and to our life with

God. Justice is neither an option or a secondary issue for us. Justice brings to fruition God's original intentions for humankind. It was love for Christ that drove William Wilberforce to tackle the hideous reality of slavery. It is love for Christ that motivates pastors and priests to stand up for the rights of the poorest throughout the world. It is a desire for pleasing God that causes many missionaries and laypeople to seek to dismantle the scandalous practice of human trafficking for the sex industry. It was love for God that transformed an inhuman, beastly mental health system to one where people are treated with dignity. There are countless other examples. God never intended that people should oppress other people or use them as objects.

It is interesting that in the Micah passage immediately following justice, loving mercy is mentioned. Justice by itself can degenerate into a harsh, judgmental form of legalism. It is interesting that God is also interested in the life of the oppressor as well as the oppressed. He longs to see them transformed rather than destroyed. I can't help but think of John Newton, who wrote *Amazing Grace*. It was the grace and mercy of God that took him from being a slave trader to following God and being a champion of the abolition of slavery. God always intended justice to be tempered by mercy. Hence, one of the beatitudes is mercy.

*Blessed are the **merciful**, for they will be shown mercy. Matt. 5:7 (emphasis mine)*

The passage in Micah then follows with the need to walk humbly with God. Humility comes from seeing yourself from God's perspective. Your greatness shrinks before Him. Your good reputation or morality reeks of selfish ambition and conceit and the voices of those you have injured drown out your boasts. Your wealth and glory seem tawdry. A clear view of God is a tremendous antidote for chutzpah and an invaluable gift. Humility opens us up not only to God, but to those around us.

*Blessed are the **poor in spirit**, for theirs is the kingdom of heaven. Matt. 5:3 (emphasis mine)*

This triad of justice, mercy and humility operate in balance and interdependence. When they are found in a person's life they work to create a contradiction, a beautiful, complex work of art. A person becomes frightening and attractive, fearsome and gently approachable, unyielding and kind. Followers of God should be frightening, fearsome, and unyielding to the oppressor; attractive, gentle and kind to the oppressed.

God gives grace to the humble, a broken and contrite spirit are precious in His sight (Psalm 51:17). Humility keeps our feet on the ground. Humility enables us to see ourselves as we really are. There are no self-made people, there is no class or race of people better than another, no person or group can claim superiority. We all benefit from the grace of God in varying degrees. None is totally self-sufficient and no one is totally independent. The least in gifts, resources and abilities is to be valued as much as the greatest. We all are expendable and we all stand or fall according to God's grace. History is full of examples of such people. One of the oldest stories of such a person is the story of Job.

Job as a model of righteous living

The story of Job is full of drama, irony, conflict, tragedy and triumph. It is fully human and gives an amazing picture of how circumstance can cloud our view of ourselves, leading nearly to despair, as well as obscure and distort our view of God.

At the beginning of the book, God declares Job to be a righteous man. Job pleases God and God brags on him to the evil one. The evil one, Satan, argues that the only reason Job follows God is that God keeps Job bribed with good things, a loving family, wealth, prestige, and a life free of calamity. To prove otherwise, God allows the evil one to touch Job's life. He loses all but his wife, who in her agony declares Job should curse God and die. Job refuses and praises God saying,

> ... *"Naked I came from my mother's womb and naked I will depart. The LORD gave and the LORD has taken away;* **may the name of the LORD be praised.**"
>
> *In all this, Job did not sin by charging God with wrongdoing. Job 1:20ff (emphasis mine)*

In his defeat the evil one argues that if Job's health were touched, if he personally, physically suffered, he would turn away from following God. The evil one is given permission and Job is devastated with illness. In his misery, he has friends come to him and argue that there must be some hidden sin Job has committed for this calamity to be upon him. If things are bad in his life, God must be mad at him. Together, the three of them chide, berate and abuse Job hoping to get him to confess to some sin. Remember, God had already declared him to be righteous. Job's friends' faulty theology was being forced upon Job, an act of arrogance, insensitivity and ignorance. Job finally decides to defend himself and demonstrate to them that he is indeed a righteous man.

> *Whoever heard me spoke well of me, and those who saw me commended me, because* **I rescued the poor who cried for help, and the fatherless who had none to assist them. Those who were dying blessed me; I made the widow's heart sing. I put on righteousness as my clothing; justice was my robe and my**

turban. I was eyes to the blind and feet to the lame.
I was a father to the needy; I took up the case of
the stranger. I broke the fangs of the wicked and
snatched the victims from their teeth. Job 29:11ff
(emphasis mine)

Job defended himself by focusing on specific acts
designed to show that he loved his neighbor as much as himself. His love of God was exhibited in his desire to help those
less fortunate, to defend the weak, to ensure justice.

Wait you say, there is nothing in those passages that
speaks of personal holiness, pure thoughts, inward devotion
to God. True. Read the full passages and you will find those
as well. The above passages are important because they
outwardly, in measurable terms, prove one's love for God.
God defines knowing Him with doing those types of things.
The inward acts are private, and some would say suspect. In
speaking to a king of Judah, God says:

"Does it make you a king to have more and more
cedar? Did not your father have food and drink? **He**
did what was right and just, so all went well with
him. He defended the cause of the poor and needy,
and so all went well. Is that not what it means to
know me?" *declares the LORD.* Jer. 22:15 *(emphasis*
mine)

The same is echoed in the New Testament. What is
God's measure of the purity of our devotion? Is it our emotion during prayer or worship? Is it the mastery of specific
doctrines? Is it our ability to overcome bad habits, to improve
ourselves? James speaks to this.

Religion that God our Father accepts as pure and
faultless is this: **to look after orphans and widows**

in their distress and to keep oneself from being polluted by the world. James. 1:27 (emphasis mine)

The recurring theme in scripture is that the soundness and quality of our devotion to God is manifest in how we treat others, especially the most vulnerable and most marginalized in our society. **Worship, church attendance, tithing, are all secondary to this.**

Jesus used this defense when the disciples of John the baptizer came to Him, asking if He was the Messiah. Here's poor John thrown into prison, wondering if the one he introduced as the Lamb of God truly was the One. "Did I make a mistake?" he thought. He wasn't out there to observe what Jesus was doing. He got all his information secondhand and not regularly. How would Jesus respond to the greatest of prophets, the one Jesus called the greatest ever born of a woman? He responds in a way that sounds much like how Job responded.

*So he replied to the messengers, "**Go back and report to John what you have seen and heard: The blind receive sight, the lame walk, those who have leprosy are cleansed, the deaf hear, the dead are raised, and the good news is proclaimed to the poor.**" Luke 7:22 (emphasis mine)*

When John heard this, I'm sure he sat back and smiled. His work was over. He recognized that what Jesus was doing was exactly what was prophesied He'd do in Isaiah 61.

Implications of living out Micah 6:8 Because the passage in Micah begins with the concept of justice, it rules out merely living out your life with God privately as a purely personal matter. To do justice implies acting in the world. It infers a responsibility for others who may be the objects of oppression, the victims of circumstance, or those suffering from the errors of others. To follow God involves living outside yourself and your immediate family. Following God expands your world.

> *"Oh, that you would bless me and **enlarge my territory**! Let your hand be with me, and keep me from harm so that I will be free from pain." And God granted his request." 1 Chronicles 4:10 (emphasis mine)*

This prayer of Jabez was less for personal gain than personal influence. He wanted his ability to influence others to follow God increased. He wanted to live larger than himself and his personal concerns. He knew through the Lord he would be able to have a life of significance, influence and impact. He knew his vision was too limited, too small, and too personal. The cry of his heart extended outside himself.

Living large with God

God calls us to be a people for Him. Not merely a person who follows Him, surely but not exclusively a family who follows Him. We are to be a People of God who call those in the world to become a people of God. Our radical individualism in the United States blinds us to the reality that the majority of times the word "you" is used in the New Testament, it is plural.

This individualism does much to distort our relationship with God and to distort what is in the scripture. How often have you heard people talk of the great promises of God available to us? Closer examination of these promises reveals they nearly all are conditional. Nearly all are linked to the advancement of His Kingdom in one way or another. The promises of God are for furthering His Kingdom, not feathering our nests. It begins with Abraham.

*"I will make you into a great nation, and I will bless you; I will make your name great, and you will be a blessing. I will bless those who bless you, and whoever curses you I will curse; **and all peoples on earth will be blessed through you.**" Gen. 12:2 (emphasis mine)*

God's promise to Abraham results in Abraham becoming a blessing to others. From the beginning God intended Abraham to be a witness of the goodness of God and the rightness of following Him. Being a witness for God in the world was a key component to being a people of God.

*May God be gracious to us and bless us and make His face shine on us so **that Your ways may be known on earth, Your salvation among all nations**. Ps. 67:1 (emphasis mine)*

In every era, in every generation, those who choose to follow God have been given responsibility to live in a manner that reveals the character of God to a world suspicious of Him. More than that, God has given those who follow Him the responsibility to demonstrate to the world God's love and the wisdom of following His direction. We are to become the catalyst for reconciliation and healing between God and humankind and between various peoples.

*All this is from God, who reconciled us to himself through Christ **and gave us the ministry of reconciliation:** that God was reconciling the world to himself in Christ, not counting people's sins against them. And he has committed to us the message of reconciliation. We are therefore Christ's ambassadors, as though God were making his appeal through us.*

*We implore you on Christ's behalf: Be reconciled to
God. 2Cor. 5:18ff (emphasis mine)*

When Jesus sent out His disciples, the charge He gave
them was holistic. It involved not only spiritual reconciliation with God, but the direct charge to begin the process
of healing and reclaiming what the evil one has sought to
destroy. All of this is based upon what God has done for us.
We embark on this quest because we are recipients of the
good things which have arisen from it.

*As you go, proclaim this message: 'The kingdom of
heaven has come near.' Heal the sick, raise the dead,
cleanse those who have leprosy, drive out demons.
Freely you have received, freely give. Matt. 10:7*

God expects those who follow him to live expansive lives,
not lives that contract into cocoons of false security and self
or "tribal" interest. God has never been a tribal God. He is
not merely interested in certain people or people groups. He
is God of the nations, of the whole world. He longs for His
message to be preached to all peoples.

*And this gospel of the kingdom will be preached in
the whole world as a testimony to all nations, and
then the end will come. Matt. 24:14*

"But", you say, "How can we live like this when we have
so many problems ourselves?"
What is amazing is that when we embrace this expansive
way of living, we find that the problems that plagued us prior
to this turn out to be smaller than they were before. They
don't feel so oppressive or controlling of our lives. Why?
Because we see them in a different perspective.

When we allow our perspective on life to be dominated by only our family, or only our personal happiness, we end up looking at the world the way one does when looking through a long hollow tube. The world is reduced to a one inch circle and the horizon and panorama of life disappear. When we open ourselves up to the world that God loves, we gain new perspective, see new options and gain the ability to focus on a broader scale and to have a much longer vision since the whole panorama is now there for consideration. The problems and difficulties that dominated our vision and overwhelmed our emotions now are shown in their smallness and simplicity in comparison to the broader, grander picture. What was colossal becomes trivial. Most people's world is too small. The smallness of that world magnifies every element within it. God made us for the reality of a large, complex, creative life. When we limit our focus to only portions of what He intended, a struggle takes place within us as the God-given tendencies within us seek to enlarge the area of our focus to meet the size of the regal stature God placed on us. We were the crown of His creation. He made us to live with Him and rule with Him (He gave us dominion over all creation as its stewards). To help us in figuring out how to live large in the world, God has given us some metaphors to consider.

How is living large translated practically?

Many times I have heard people speak with frustration about the parables of Jesus. Why didn't He just come out and say what He wanted to say? A list of rules would be so much easier. The problem with a list of rules is that they are so static, inflexible, and lifeless, unable to address the myriad of problems and convolutions in which we find ourselves in the real world. Instead, He gives metaphors and stories that illuminate His will, expecting us to use the creativity He placed within us, guided by the Holy Spirit, to interpret and create a unique application of the principles in the metaphor or story.

This to me is wonderful. God expects me to be sensitive to the Holy Spirit and creatively apply the principles in my context, constrained by circumstances unique to me. What trust God places in us! What are the broad principles he outlines for living large in the world?

Small is beautiful

Never despise the day of small beginnings. Too often we paralyze ourselves from acting by thinking we need to do the hero's feat. The American way of thinking is big, grandiose. The parable of Bigger Barns in Luke is a truly American parable. The liberating truth is that we need not worry about the big deeds, we instead, as Mother Theresa stated, must learn to do small things with great love. I tell people all the time that 90% is just showing up.

> *He told them another parable: "The kingdom of heaven is like a **mustard seed**, which a man took and planted in his field. **Though it is the smallest** of all seeds, yet when it grows, it is the largest of garden plants and becomes a tree, so that the birds come and perch in its branches." Matt. 13:31 (emphasis mine)*

It's not the size of the deed but the quality of the deed, just as it's not the size of the seed that's important. When we begin to do small things with great love, we put in motion a process that God will bring to fruition. He may take our small deed and grow it large so major sections of society benefit from it. He may merely plant it deeply in the heart of a person and use it to energize His word, leading to salvation and transformation. However God seeks to use the deeds we perform, we must remember that unless we die to the deed, it will not germinate and grow.

> *Very truly I tell you,* **unless a kernel of wheat falls to the ground and dies, it remains only a single seed.** *But if it dies, it produces many seeds.* **Those who love their life will lose it,** *while those who hate their life in this world will keep it for eternal life. Jn. 12:24 (emphasis mine)*

All too often the deeds we are supposedly doing unto the Lord are actually done to enrich ourselves. We act in order to fill some inner need of acceptance, self-esteem, or self or public validation through performance. While doing the deed, we expect to receive back gratitude from the recipient, recognition from our peers or have some expectation of change or achievement met. When these don't appear, we often become angry, question whether or not we should continue, or pass judgment on the action or recipient. What these responses reveal is that we are not serving God or the recipient of our actions, but ourselves. We must die to these expectations and focus only on doing small things with great love. When the deed is done fully as unto the Lord, our dying to personal gratification, recognition, and achievement releases the act into God's hands to do with as He sees fit. When that happens, the possibility for miraculous results opens up. We needn't fret over whether or not our service is in vain. When done properly, it has eternal consequences.

I believe that whatever we begin in the Lord's name now to advance the Kingdom will ultimately be brought to fullness when the Kingdom fully arrives at Jesus' return. He will look at us and say, "Remember when you tried to overcome that evil in your area and became frustrated because you couldn't get the resources or responses you prayed for? Well, here's all you need, go and accomplish it now, only this time, you are sure to succeed." I believe we can't fail and that nothing we do is inconsequential when done in the power of the Spirit and in obedience to God.

The passage also tells me this truth. Remember earlier when I mentioned that wherever you are, there the Kingdom of God exists in fullness? This parable points to that. God planted you where you are. Your first mission field is all around you. It is good to go on short-term mission trips, but your true effectiveness will be in the vineyard God has placed you in; your neighborhood, your school, your place of employment, your club or small group. Wherever you go, there you are...an ambassador of Christ in the place He has put you. This parable of the kernel of wheat speaks to that.

Life in you transforms life around you

You needn't worry if you will be required to become a professional religionist. I firmly believe that God wants us to live out the unique gifts and abilities He has entrusted to us in creative ways in our communities. This means that your abilities and interests in sports, business, politics, the arts, music, academics, and any other areas are to become tools of advancing God's Kingdom. They are not the focus, they are merely tools to allow the Life in the Spirit God placed within you to be expressed and affect every aspect of life in our communities. We are to become like yeast.

*He told them still another parable: "The kingdom of heaven is like **yeast** that a woman took and mixed into about sixty pounds of **flour until it worked all through the dough.**" Matt. 13:33 (emphasis mine)*

I believe that every strata in society needs to be permeated with the presence of God, in the same manner that yeast permeates bread. We need people producing excellent movies from a Christian worldview, we need Christian scientists affecting how we view genetic research, we need politicians who will function from a Christian worldview. Nearly every profession, and nearly every leisure activity needs the presence of a committed Christian, living out the teachings of Jesus with sensitivity and wisdom, protecting those who are marginalized and being a voice for those who have no voice.

When we place ourselves at the disposal of Christ in our daily lives, we transform the mundane into the holy. We inject the presence of God and His interest into every aspect of life to be expressed through us. When we live in a manner free of condemnation and judgment, allowing the Holy Spirit to minister grace to those around us, we will find that co-workers will begin to be affected by the integrity, compassion, kindness and gentleness present when we walk in the Spirit. Nothing changes perceptions about religion, answers criticisms of narrow mindedness, hatefulness, or intellectual questions like a life lived in the power of the Holy Spirit. When we give God access to all our interests and all our ambitions, when we allow Him to live through us wherever we are, we release His power to advance His Kingdom and lay claim to every place our foot falls as part of His Kingdom.

It is this willingness to become a channel for God's blessing and presence that enables His power to affect the world. Responding to Him in love and allowing Him to transform our character to be in conformity with the fruits of the Spirit, mentioned in Galatians 5, adds a flavor to our life which is attractive to people. Our life with Christ acts as a spice in an otherwise bland existence without God.

A little goes a long way

Jesus drew attention to the unique role His followers play in society. He likened us to one of the most valuable and necessary spices in His day.

*"**You are the salt of the earth**. But if the salt loses its saltiness, how can it be made salty again? It is no longer good for anything, except to be thrown out and trampled underfoot." Matt. 5:13 (emphasis mine)*

This metaphor gives insight into what it means to hunger and thirst for justice. One role we play involves restraining evil. The Bible makes it clear that the Holy Spirit acts as a restraining force, holding back the powers of darkness. Since we are the body of Christ, the Holy Spirit uses us as His hands and feet to accomplish the task.

Another role we play is preserving what is good and seeing to it that all benefit from it. We have not only a negative role, but a positive one. It is through our actions and testimony that the person and character of God are made known in the world.

Let your conversation be always full of grace, seasoned with salt, so that you may know how to answer everyone. Colossians 4:6 (emphasis mine)

The way we live, and what we say, should serve to whet people's appetite for a life lived in communion with God. The passage implies calculated restraint in terms of vocal witness. Just as too much salt spoils the natural flavor of food, the unhealthy application of a verbal witness serves to assault the sensibilities of people. They need to also be able to examine the deeds we do which give life and credibility to our words. Action and testimony artfully woven together are virtually unassailable witness to the truth of the Gospel.

Just as yeast must be worked into the dough, permeating it, so too salt is worthless unless similarly applied. Salt in the salt shaker is merely a promise of flavor or preservation. For all intents and purposes, it is worthless if left there and forgotten. When salt loses its saltiness, it becomes truly worthless. Hidden in this metaphor is a warning to maintain vital connectedness to the King, to allow His principles of living to direct and shape our lives. Our saltiness comes from the transformation of the Spirit as our desires, ambitions, thoughts and plans come into alignment with God's.

As we permeate society and bring to bear His principles for living, rooted in a sense of justice, we begin to open eyes currently focused on personal gratification and personal ambition to a more humane way of living. It's as if a light were turned on in a room.

The smallest light defeats the greatest darkness

I remember when our kids were little, taking them into an old abandoned copper mine. We didn't go in far, just far enough so that when we turned off our lights, the darkness was so dense that you couldn't see your hand in front of your face. Then, just by striking a little match, the whole tunnel would light up. Small lights should not be seen as insignificant.

I am always surprised when I hear fellow followers of Christ speak in fear of evil. I believe it is an affront to God to cower and worry about evil. I have spoken with countless followers of Jesus who have shared their terrors and phobias after reading about demons, seeing a movie about an exorcism, or relating how the latest news story has caused them to feel less secure or merely more vulnerable. Granted, I can understand concern and the need to practice vigilance, but to allow these fears to paralyze and control you to the point of disengaging from the world denies the resurrection power of Christ.

*You, dear children, are from God and have overcome them, because the **one** (the Holy Spirit) **who is in you*** *is greater than the one who is in the world* (the evil one). 1 John 4:4 (emphasis mine)

Jesus declares that we are the light of the world, set on display to show the way to others. We show the way to God while at the same time revealing the futility and self-destructive nature of living a life without God.

"You are the light of the world. A city on a hill cannot be hidden. Neither do people light a lamp and put it under a bowl. Instead they put it on its stand, and it gives light to everyone in the house. In the same way, let your light shine before others, that they may see your good deeds and glorify your Father in heaven." Matt. 5:14 (emphasis mine)

Light is only good when it is used in darkness. We show the way to God, we are the role models. Too often we run from the darkness. Do we believe that light is greater than darkness? We should run TO the darkness. Where are those dark places in our cities and towns? Where are the areas needing the presence and deliverance of the Lord? They are easier to find than you think. When we walk in the Light as He is in the light, our eyes are opened to suffering, oppression, loneliness, manipulation and exploitation that exist in the world. They may be manifest in our deepest ghettos or richest gated communities. Those who halfheartedly follow Jesus are able to look at the world around them but they are seldom able to really see that world and the forces shaping the people in it. To wholeheartedly follow, to be willing to obey Christ when He directs us to act, enables us to fully comprehend the bondage and need for deliverance. It is these people who will fulfill the greatest command

"'Love the Lord your God with all your heart and with all your soul and with all your strength and with all your mind;' and, 'Love your neighbor as your-self.'" Luke 10:27 (emphasis mine)

I John 3:16-18 is as important as John 3:16-18

The question always arises as to who our neighbor is, just as Jesus encountered in this passage in Luke. People often want to stay around those just like themselves or people who are above them in class or income (upward mobility is always more attractive than downward mobility.) *"Doesn't God care for the rich as well? Some of their lives are really messed up."* Yes, I tell them, but God has made it a point to identify specific groups of people He feels need special attention and with whom we should be regularly involved. God feels so strongly about these people that He personally identifies with them to the point that when you help them, hurt them, or ignore them, He feels you are dealing directly with Him. Who are these people?

*"Do not mistreat or oppress a **foreigner**, for you were foreigners in Egypt. "Do not take advantage of a **widow** or an **orphan**. If you do and they cry out to me, I will certainly hear their cry. My anger will be aroused, and I will kill you with the sword; your wives will become widows and your children father-less." Ex. 22:21 (emphasis mine)*

*Those who are kind to the **poor** lend to the LORD, and he will reward them for what they have done. Prov. 19:17 (emphasis mine)*

*Those who shut their ears to the **cry of the poor**
will also cry out and not be answered. Prov. 21:13
(emphasis mine)*

*There will always be poor people in the land.
Therefore I command you to **be openhanded toward
those of your people who are poor and needy** in your
land. Deut. 15:11 (emphasis mine)*

I think you get it by now. These are just a few of the hundreds of verses which speak of God's special connection to the marginalized and most vulnerable in society. When our hearts are captured by the heart of God, our hearts reflect the burdens and affections of His heart. We begin to champion those issues which are near to the heart of God. In a very real way we become His advocates for justice in the world, we

*Speak up for those who cannot speak for themselves,
for the rights of all who are destitute. Speak up and
judge fairly; defend the rights of the poor and needy.
Prov. 31:8*

Our lives begin to reflect His agenda in the world. We are not recognized as being merely religious, "pie in the sky" people, but activists who seek to promote justice, righteousness, and peace in the world. We begin to fulfill the admonition of God through the prophet Isaiah

*"Is not this the kind of fasting I have chosen: **to loose
the chains of injustice and untie the cords of the
yoke, to set the oppressed free and break every yoke?
Is it not to share your food with the hungry and to
provide the poor wanderer with shelter— when you
see the naked, to clothe them, and not to turn away
from your own flesh and blood?"** Isa. 58:6*

__Then__ your light will break forth like the dawn, and your healing will quickly appear; I will go before you, and the glory of the LORD will be your rear guard. __Then__ you will call, and the LORD will answer; you will cry for help, and he will say: Here am I. If you do away with the yoke of oppression, with the pointing finger and malicious talk, and __if you spend yourselves in behalf of the hungry and satisfy the needs of the oppressed, then__ your light will rise in the darkness, and your night will become like the noonday. The LORD will guide you always; he will satisfy your needs in a sun-scorched land and will strengthen your frame. You will be like a well-watered garden, like a spring whose waters never fail. Your people will rebuild the ancient ruins and will raise up the age-old foundations; __you will be called Repairer of Broken Walls, Restorer of Streets with Dwellings__. Isa. 58:8 (emphasis mine)

We will fulfill Jesus' command in scripture in wonderfully creative ways by doing things like throwing parties for the poor, disabled, blind, and others who are often pushed to the periphery of society,

"When you give a luncheon or dinner, do not invite your friends, your brothers or sisters, your relatives, or your rich neighbors; if you do, they may invite you back and so you will be repaid. But when you give a banquet, __invite the poor, the crippled, the lame, the blind, and you will be blessed.__ Although they cannot repay you, you will be repaid at the resurrection of the righteous." Luke 14:12 (emphasis mine)

We demonstrate to the world not only God's amazing love and grace, but how following Him actually turns us into winsome, creative, compassionate people. This is greatly needed in a time when we are more often seen as being more closed, dispassionate and restrictive in our culture.

The expression of your obedience will be a combination of your own creativity and interests directed by the Holy Spirit according to God's priorities and utilizing the unique gifts God entrusted to you and each person in your family. The problem will not be trying to figure out what to do, but trying to limit your focus so that you are not spread too thin in terms of time and resources. Potential areas of interest bombard us in news broadcasts, magazines, movies, radio programs, and other forms of mass media. There are local needs at homeless shelters, orphanages, unwed mother shelters, after school tutoring programs and countless other social/human needs crying for remedy. Internationally the prospects increase in seeming exponential fashion. Modern slavery begs abolition, the images of refugees should break our hearts, human trafficking, brutalizing poverty, child exploitation, rampant treatable diseases going untreated due to lack of funding, the scandalous treatment of women and young girls in so many cultures, and I can go on and on. We live in a world crying out for help. Families who wish to embody the life of presence of God will have to limit their involvement to one or two major areas of focus.

Summary

The purposes of God are revealed in the character of God. Our purposes reveal our character. God has a heart for those who have been left behind, for those who are lost, for those who are hurting or struggling, for the marginalized in society. He loves them so much that He left heaven and came to dwell among them, purchasing their salvation with His own blood and suffering.

He has declared His priorities throughout scripture. He has zeroed in on widows, orphans, the poor, the oppressed, and the immigrant/stranger as special groups of people with whom He uniquely identifies.

He has placed the quest for justice, mercy and humility at the center of life with Him. To seek after these is to resonate with His Heart. He uses attention to these as a measure of our love for Him.

To be strong for Jesus...you must be strong for the poor.

Our family has a missions budget. *We are able to do a lot in terms of family involvement. We don't have a few monumental events, rather, it's continual, consistent and focused times that we see results from. Many of these times are spontaneous and very unplanned (much like childhood is). We get letters from missionaries and get out maps to see where they are. When the missionaries return we visit with them and sometimes plan trips to help them. This proved to be life-changing for all our kids. They all cleaned out their closets and gave away clothes for the needy when they returned home. In looking back on this I have to say that there was not one defining moment or event that shaped our kid's lives. It was the life-style we quietly lived daily. It was our living out our commitment for them daily that made the difference. They are now all grown and involved in churches and community outreach.*

Our family purpose statement is ***"We will tell the next generation the praiseworthy deeds of the Lord, and they in turn will tell their children, then they would put their trust in God."*** *Psalm 78:4-7 We put it in calligraphy on the wall in the dining room. Our 3 ½ year old granddaughter looked at it the other day while eating lunch and we had a great conversation about what it meant.*

Debbie, GA

Chapter 6

Faithing as a family activity

When you look at God's Kingdom plan and your role in it, you can be overwhelmed. What is essential to remember is that it will take faith, or rather, faithing. I like to think of faith as a verb, an action, rather than a noun, something you can possess. Faithing is something you do. God likes faithing, He looks for it in those who follow Him and He rewards those who practice it. Faithing is the currency of the Kingdom. Through it all the work in the Kingdom is accomplished. By faithing our life, we tap into the power and resources of God, bringing infinite influence to bear on finite problems and challenges. Faithing is anchored in a confidence in God. Our knowledge of Him is bolstered through countless acts of obedience, myriad examples of His dependability and provision, and strengthened through the avalanche of trials and tribulation. Because He has proven Himself able to deliver in seemingly insurmountable circumstances, we should be emboldened to act in ways that our culture would consider unwise, irresponsible, reckless or outrageous. Faithing enables us to break through the veil of our finite existence and embrace eternity. Faithing changes uncertainties and obstacles into visions of a new future and opportunities for God to transform us and those around us.

God has declared in His word that

...the righteous will live by his faithing (my emphasis).
Hab. 2:4

But my righteous one will live by faithing. Heb. 10:38
(change to faithing mine)

There are a lot of misconceptions about faith floating around out there. For me, one of the first I had to confront was that when you are faithing, you are absent of fear or apprehension. I remember when God called me to start Mustard Seeds and Mountains to work among the poor in Appalachia. The task seemed so large and the obstacles so huge that I felt I would not have the faith to be successful. I never entertained the idea of not doing what God wanted, of not obeying and following through. I just felt that somehow I didn't have what it took. I felt that merely because I was experiencing fear and apprehension, I lacked any faith. I met with John Perkins, a leader in racial reconciliation and community development, to share my concerns and get his input. He shared with me that the presence of fear or apprehension does not indicate anything other than the immensity of the task. The test is whether or not you move ahead in spite of the concerns. He shared how he too has had to faith through a landscape of challenges often unsure of how or what God was going to do. What I learned is that fear and apprehension can be useful modifiers of faithing if they don't freeze us into a state of inaction. While they can be companions of faithing, they really are part of the landscape that those of us faithing must traverse, the ever present scenery which can be viewed in two ways-as both an amazing landscape and backdrop for God's work or insurmountable obstacles to it. What makes the difference is whether or not they are our focus. For faithing, the focus must be upon the Lord and His call to action. It is God and His ability brought to bear through our actions which will determine the outcome.

As people of the Kingdom, we must become thoroughly familiar with the character of God, how He deals with those who follow Him, and His plans for the world. For this reason, it is imperative that we be people of prayer and Bible study.

> *Consequently,* **faith comes from hearing the message**, *and the message is heard through the word of Christ. Rom. 10:17*

Saturating our minds with knowledge of God and how He dealt with people in the past gives us insights into the character and nature of God that helps squelch momentary fears and apprehensions. We develop a confidence in what God will do based upon our knowledge of what He has done. The stories of the Old and New Testaments take on new meaning and significance when looked at through the lens of faithing.

> *The LORD had said to Abram, "Leave your country, your people and your father's household and go to the land I will show you. "I will make you into a great nation and I will bless you; I will make your name great, and you will be a blessing. I will bless those who bless you, and whoever curses you I will curse; and all peoples on earth will be blessed* **through** *you."*

> **So Abram left, as the LORD had told him;** *and Lot went with him. Abram was seventy-five years old when he set out from Haran. He took his wife Sarai, his nephew Lot, all the possessions they had accu-*

mulated and the people they had acquired in Haran, and they set out for the land of Canaan, and they arrived there. Gen. 12:1-4

*By faith(ing) Abraham, when called to go to a place he would later receive as his inheritance, **obeyed and went,** even though he did not know where he was going. By faith(ing) he made his home in the Promised Land like a stranger in a foreign country; he lived in tents, as did Isaac and Jacob, who were heirs with him of the same promise. For he was looking forward to the city with foundations, whose architect and builder is God. Heb. 11:8 (emphasis and addition of "ing" to faith mine)*

Abraham was able to take a journey into uncertainty because he had a personal knowledge of God and relationship with Him. Because of this relationship and the passion which grew out of it, Abraham was able to do what seemed scary indeed. Abraham had already anchored his heart to God's heart, not in his possessions, his people, or his place of origin. His passion was God, and when God revealed His specific will to him, Abraham acted.

Seeing faith as a verb plants your feet firmly on the Rock. God addresses the misconception of faith as an intellectual or mental state versus an action in the book of James.

What good is it, my brothers, if a man claims to have faith but has no deeds? Can such faith save him? Suppose a brother or sister is without clothes and daily food. If one of you says to him, "Go, I wish you well; keep warm and well fed," but does nothing about his physical needs, what good is it? In the same way, faith by itself, if it is not accompanied by action, is dead.

*...You foolish man, do you want evidence that **faith without deeds is useless?** Was not our ancestor Abraham considered righteous **for what he did** when he offered his son Isaac on the altar? You see that his **faith and his actions were working together,** and his **faith was made complete by what he did.** And the scripture was fulfilled that says, "Abraham believed God, and it was credited to him as righteousness," and he was called God's friend. You see that a person is justified by what he does and not by faith alone. James 2:14-22 (emphasis mine)*

Quite simply, those who "have faith" are those who are doing something in obedience. It is those who act on the promises of God as though there were no way they could not be fulfilled. That's why it is not the size of faith that is important, but its very active expression that is essential. The disciples wanted Jesus to treat faith as a thing, which in their minds needed to be a certain size to be effective (increase our faith). His response was to say, it's not the size that's important, but the fact that it's active that must be grasped. Faith is not a thing to possess or hold but a thing to use. It is so powerful, so concentrated, that once unleashed, it can move mountains (Matt. 17:20).

Faithing acts as a window into what we really think and feel about God. Like a barometer, it measures our true devotion to God. God sees faithing as evidence of our allegiance to Him. Faithing is made evident, real, through our acts of obedience and through our attempts to advance God's Kingdom. He gives most of us great latitude in how this faithing is to be expressed in our lives, letting us choose areas of service. Sometimes He becomes very specific and calls certain ones of us to specific work full-time in order to advance the Kingdom. Most of the time, He allows us to choose. He leads us into green pastures, but doesn't tell us every blade of grass to eat.

When you begin to embark on the journey of making mission and advancing God's Kingdom a matter of lifestyle rather than periodic activity, you too will be faced with trials and challenges which will test the loyalty of your heart. Where is your heart anchored? What is most precious to you? Look at the test God placed before Abraham and his family.

Some time later God tested Abraham. He said to him, "Abraham!"

*"Here I am," he replied. Then God said, **"Take your son, your only son, Isaac, whom you love, and go to the region of Moriah. Sacrifice him there as a burnt offering** on one of the mountains I will tell you about."*

Early the next morning Abraham got up and saddled his donkey. He took with him two of his servants and his son Isaac. When he had cut enough wood for the burnt offering, he set out for the place God had told him about. On the third day Abraham looked up and saw the place in the distance. He said to his servants, "Stay here with the donkey while I and the boy go over there. We will worship and then we will come back to you."

Abraham took the wood for the burnt offering and placed it on his son Isaac, and he himself carried the fire and the knife. As the two of them went on together, Isaac spoke up and said to his father Abraham, "Father?"

"Yes, my son?" Abraham replied.

"The fire and wood are here," Isaac said, "but where is the lamb for the burnt offering?"

Abraham answered, **"God himself will provide the lamb for the burnt offering, my son." And the two of them went on together. When they reached the place God had told him about, Abraham built an altar there and arranged the wood on it. He bound his son Isaac and laid him on the altar, on top of the wood. Then he reached out his hand and took the knife to slay his son.** *But the angel of the LORD called out to him from heaven, "Abraham! Abraham!"*

"Here I am," he replied.

"Do not lay a hand on the boy," he said. **"Do not do anything to him. Now I know that you fear God, because you have not withheld from me your son, your only son."** *Gen. 22:1ff (emphasis mine)*

This portion of scripture strikes at the foundations of Abraham's knowledge of God; his understanding of what it meant to be a good parent; and his expectations regarding God's promises. He must confront his aspirations of being seen as a model parent, or community member; and his self-image. It equally challenges Isaac's understanding of his father's role and relationship to him, his trust in his father, his understanding of God and what God requires of those who follow Him, and his personal aspirations for the future and God's plan for him.

God's demand of Abraham set in motion three days of soul searching and struggle. **Note that Abraham rose early the next day to begin to obey what God wanted him to do.**

Then for three days he traveled with his son and servants to the mount of murder (for that was what he was asked to do). I imagine that those must have been some silent and intense days, as Abraham had to die to notions he had nurtured and cherished about himself, God, and his future. It must have been three days of deep examination and reflection on the person and character of God. It also set in motion three days of confusion for Isaac as he tried to understand what God had called his father to do. Isaac knew the preparations for sacrifice but saw no sacrificial animal. I imagine too that he was concerned over the silence of his father and his intense brooding (no mention is made of any questions being asked regarding the trip or the task). He may have felt a tinge of fear or apprehension.

At the end of the three days, Abraham had come to some conclusions based upon how God had dealt with him in the past and what God had revealed about Himself in promises and interactions. Abraham was certain God would either provide another sacrifice or raise Isaac from the dead once the sacrifice was complete.

> *By faith Abraham, when God tested him, offered Isaac as a sacrifice. He who had received the promises was about to sacrifice his one and only son, even though God had said to him, "It is through Isaac that your offspring will be reckoned."* **Abraham reasoned that God could raise the dead**, *and figuratively speaking, he did receive Isaac back from death. Heb. 11:17 (emphasis mine)*

God stays Abraham's hand and reveals a replacement for the boy. God then praises Abraham for his faithing (obedience), his demonstration of love and devotion to God. For this act, Abraham goes down in history as the father of all those who are faithers.

When we begin to place love of God and the advancement of His Kingdom at the heart of our lives and families, we can be certain that we will be asked to live a faithing life. God will require us to say and do things not required of others, because God is confident that we will act on His command. We can be sure that we will embark on adventures others never encounter. We can also be certain that we will gain a knowledge of and communion with God that others only read about. Our faithing, our obedience burns like sweet smelling incense and rises to the highest heavens to the nostrils of God. God delights in those who live by faithing. He draws near those who are bold enough to attempt things worthy of His name.

The scriptures are full of places where God delights in those who are faithing. Here is one place where we find Jesus astonished (God being astonished...imagine) at the faith He encounters.

When Jesus had entered Capernaum, a centurion came to him, asking for help. "Lord," he said, "my servant lies at home paralyzed and in terrible suffering."

Jesus said to him, "I will go and heal him."

The centurion replied, "Lord, I do not deserve to have you come under my roof. But just say the word, and my servant will be healed. For I myself am a man under authority, with soldiers under me. I tell this one, 'Go,' and he goes; and that one, 'Come,' and he comes. I say to my servant, 'Do this,' and he does it."

When Jesus heard this, he was astonished and said to those following him, "I tell you the truth, I have

not found anyone in Israel with such great faith.
*I say to you that many will come from the east and
the west, and will take their places at the feast with
Abraham, Isaac and Jacob in the kingdom of heaven.
But the subjects of the kingdom will be thrown outside,
into the darkness, where there will be weeping and
gnashing of teeth." Then Jesus said to the centurion,
"Go! It will be done just as you believed it would."
And his servant was healed at that very hour. Matt.
8:5ff (emphasis mine)*

In another story, Jesus is so moved by the faith of friends
helping their sick comrade that He goes beyond physical
healing to forgiving the man's sins. In the process, He demonstrates to all that He has power to forgive sins, something
only God can do.

*Jesus stepped into a boat, crossed over and came
to his own town. Some men brought to him a paralytic, lying on a mat.* **When Jesus saw their faith,** *he
said to the paralytic, "Take heart, son; your sins are
forgiven."*

*At this, some of the teachers of the law said to them-
selves, "This fellow is blaspheming!"*

*Knowing their thoughts, Jesus said, "Why do you
entertain evil thoughts in your hearts? Which is
easier: to say, 'Your sins are forgiven,' or to say,
'Get up and walk'? But so that you may know that
the Son of Man has authority on earth to forgive sins.
. . ." Then he said to the paralytic, "Get up, take
your mat and go home." And the man got up and
went home. When the crowd saw this, they were filled*

with awe; and they praised God, who had given such authority to men. Matt. 9:1ff (emphasis mine)

Personally, one of my favorite sections deals with Stephen preaching to the Jews. After Pentecost, tension had been building in Jerusalem as the Jewish leaders were trying to figure out what to do with these followers of Jesus. People had been awed by displays of God's healing, judgment, and work among Jesus' followers. Thousands were joining their church. Stephen is singled out by the Jews as one of their key leaders and confronted. Stephen, through the Holy Spirit, boldly speaks God's word and calls the listeners to repent and believe in Christ (a great example of faithing).

When they heard this, they were furious and gnashed their teeth at him. But Stephen, full of the Holy Spirit, looked up to heaven and saw the glory of God, and Jesus standing at the right hand of God. **"Look," he said, "I see heaven open and the Son of Man standing at the right hand of God."**

At this they covered their ears and, yelling at the top of their voices, they all rushed at him, dragged him out of the city and began to stone him. Meanwhile, the witnesses laid their clothes at the feet of a young man named Saul. **While they were stoning him, Stephen prayed, "Lord Jesus, receive my spirit." Then he fell on his knees and cried out, "Lord, do not hold this sin against them." When he had said this, he fell asleep.** *Acts 7:54ff (emphasis mine)*

In the book of Ephesians, it says that Jesus, after the resurrection, was *seated* at the right hand of God.

...which he exerted in Christ when he raised him from the dead and **seated him at his right hand in the heavenly realms,** *far above all rule and authority, power and dominion, and every title that can be given, not only in the present age but also in the one to come. Eph.1: 20 (emphasis mine)*

Stephen sees Him *standing* at the right hand of God. I believe Jesus saw Stephen boldly proclaiming the gospel to a hostile crowd. Stephen's act of faith, obedience and allegiance to Christ so impressed Jesus that He stood up. When Jesus stands up, I believe all heaven stands up. I see armies of angels watching the unfolding drama immediately stand and draw swords. All heaven's eyes focus on Christ...what is He going to do? Angels wonder, *"Is this when we ultimately put down this rebellion of the super monkeys? Will the Christ now fully implement the Kingdom?"* Millions of angel lungs fill with air for the battle cry... *"Worthy is the Lamb..."* When Jesus turns and says, *"Do you see that?! That's what I'm talking about!!!! There is some faith!! Stephen...enter into the joy prepared for you. I stand to honor and welcome you! Well done you good and faithful servant."*

This is what believers everywhere should live for. Our lives should have the aim of making the Man of Sorrows (Isa. 53:3) joyful. I personally long to hear... Well done you good and faithful servant.

What can we expect when we live in this manner?

...who through faith conquered kingdoms, administered justice, and gained what was promised; who shut the mouths of lions, quenched the fury of the flames, and escaped the edge of the sword; whose weakness was turned to strength; and who became powerful in battle and routed foreign armies. Women received back their dead, raised to life again. Others

*were tortured and refused to be released, so that they might gain a better resurrection. Some faced jeers and flogging, while still others were chained and put in prison. They were stoned; they were sawed in two; they were put to death by the sword. They went about in sheepskins and goatskins, destitute, persecuted and mistreated- **the world was not worthy of them**. They wandered in deserts and mountains, and in caves and holes in the ground.*

***These were all commended for their faith**, yet none of them received what had been promised. God had planned something better for us so that only together with us would they be made perfect. Heb. 11:33ff (emphasis mine)*

There will be victories and there will be defeats. There will be miracles in both. There will be bold manifestations of the presence of God to those who choose to faith their way through life. They will see Jesus when others don't (just like Stephen). I think the following poem captures this well.

My orders are to fight;
Then if I bleed, or fail,
Or strongly win, what matters it?
God only doth prevail.

The servant craveth naught
Except to serve with might.
I was not told to win or lose,–
My orders are to fight. Ethelwyn Wetherald

God's promises and faithing

It is possible to move forward in faith because our actions are backed by the myriad of God's promises. There has been a great misunderstanding regarding the promises of God. We often grasp them in times of difficulty like a magical amulet that is supposed to somehow force God to act in a manner which helps us. We use them like lucky charms, to ward off evil (well at least the thoughts and fears). It saddens me when I hear someone take a promise out of context and "claim" it for getting some trinket, gadget or other self-serving thing. That is nothing more than Christian witchcraft or superstition.

If you look closely, you'll discover that nearly all the promises of God are conditional. God says if you do this, I will do that. In order for the promise to kick in, we have to meet the conditions of the promise. Nearly always, the promises are directed toward those who are actively following God and seeking to advance His Kingdom. They focus on those whose hearts are in tune with the heart of God. Remember, as I previously said, the promises of God are for furthering His Kingdom, not feathering our nests.

How then does a family begin to embark on this faithing journey?

One of the most powerful ways involves prayer. Most of us have heard the old saying, "The family that prays together, stays together". Well, it just so happens that prayer is one of the key practices in faithing your life. Prayer is the language of the Kingdom and it is the primary means by which we recalibrate our hearts to resonate with the heart of God. Jesus assumes that it will be a major part of our life.

*"And **when you pray**...*

*"This, then, is **how** you should pray:*

*"'Our Father in heaven, hallowed be your name, **your kingdom come, your will be done on earth as it***

is in heaven. Give us today our daily bread. Forgive us our debts, as we also have forgiven our debtors. And lead us not into temptation, but deliver us from the evil one.' Matt. 6:5ff (emphasis mine)

Note that as we pray, we pray that God's Kingdom and will be made real upon the earth. When praying this, our will and our desires become secondary to God's.

I know, right now you may have that guilty feeling. Many people feel guilty about prayer because they don't do it, other than in a perfunctory manner. Many people see prayer as some last resort, a kind of spiritual pacifier to use when all real effort fails. Believers don't take prayer seriously and engage in it more because they don't really believe in the God that answers prayer.

Yet, there are so many passages that reveal prayer to be essential to faithing.

*"I tell you the truth, whatever you bind on earth will be bound in heaven, and whatever you loose on earth will be loosed in heaven. Again, I tell you **that if two of you on earth agree about anything you ask for, it will be done for you by my Father in heaven. For where two or three come together in my name, there am I with them.**" Matt. 18:18*

*"So I say to you: **Ask and it will be given to you; seek and you will find; knock and the door will be opened to you.**" Luke 11:9*

*I tell you the truth, **anyone who has faith in me will do what I have been doing.** He will do even greater things than these, because I am going to the Father. **And I will do whatever you ask in my name, so that the Son may bring glory to the Father. You may ask*** *me for anything in my name, and I will do it. John 14:12 (emphasis mine)*

The truth in these verses is so clear. Prayer is foundational to the advancement of the Kingdom. What is so wonderful is that anyone can pray, from the oldest to the youngest, from the strongest to the weakest, from the healthiest to the one suffering the most. Prayer is the first and most crucial step in the activities of faithing. Prayer links the finite to the infinite. Prayer is the elemental means by which we focus and apply the resources of the Kingdom of God on destroying the works of the devil.

First the prayer, then the work

The temptation is to rush into the work. That's because change brought about by our own efforts is initially much more tangible and satisfying. However, it is transitory. If the spiritual emphasis is overlooked or left out, we end up merely participating in social work. If we only pray, we end up with a false piety and, according to James, merely the decomposing shell of a living faith. Mother Teresa spoke of "praying the work", co-joining prayer and action so that they are seamless, unified activities. Then our actions reverberate through eternity and make lasting, transformational change more possible.

I remember when our children were young; we would join together in prayer for peoples around the world. We would pray for current political unrest, famines, wars, refugees, all discovered on the front pages of newspapers. Prayer went from being a formal recital of a memorized script, to the outpouring of the heart beseeching God to act in the world. I can see our 8 year old praying fervently for those suffering in Kampuchea (during the time of the killing fields), our 6 year old praying for children in the poor community in which we worked. I remember the excitement when we observed answers to our prayers.

Praying together for the world and our community had profound effects on each family member. Our prayers, over time, changed from being focused only on God alleviating discomfort in our lives, health issues for family and friends, and personal desires, to intercessory prayers. It's powerful to hear your children pray for their friends, for missionaries around the world, for believers in other parts of the world who are suffering. Next, we began to change in relation to our expectations about how God deals with us. Our praying changed our perspective on what it means to be a follower of Jesus and what is expected of one. Our praying changed the very desires of our hearts. It's difficult to go to God and pray for a new Ipod when you just spent time praying for believers in another part of the world to have food. Our praying changed the resonance of our hearts. Rather than resonating with the American Dream and conspicuous consumption (I want it all and I want it now), our hearts were tuned to the heart of God, the plight of His people in the world, and how we could make a difference, even in small ways.

Our prayers also had a role in keeping our hearts soft and our attitudes right. Often the people you serve aren't grateful or even civil to you. Their scramble for basic living needs has trained them to be grasping and aggressive. It's easy to develop resentment, anger or become disheartened, when the focus is on the behavior of those we serve. Prayer takes us back into the presence of God where the oil of His Spirit softens and soothes our hearts and attitudes. Prayer reminds us that our reward is from God, not those we serve. Our audience is God Himself, not anyone else. We minister to Jesus in a strange disguise and every encounter is a test of how well the fruits of the Spirit have taken root and grown in us.

We learned to "pray the work". We learned to do the work for Jesus, to Jesus, with Jesus, by the power of Jesus in us. The mundane was transformed into the miraculous by consciously practicing the presence of God.

Runnin' to the darkness…

Risk is at the heart of faithing. *The greater the risk you take, the more you forsake, the greater God's Kingdom you make*, is a theme we have printed on T-shirts sold by our ministry. It's distressing that somewhere along the line, the idea that God exists for our comfort took root as a major theme in Christianity. Mark Galli, in his book, *Jesus Mean and Wild*, effectively demolishes this fallacy by forcing a careful and fresh look at passages that often don't make the podium on Sundays in our seeker-focused churches (despite Jesus having spoken this to seekers). God seeks to call to Himself a people who will advance His Kingdom and destroy the works of the devil as they mimic the master who bought them with His blood.

> *He who does what is sinful is of the devil, because the devil has been sinning from the beginning. **The reason the Son of God appeared was to destroy the devil's work**. 1 John 3:8*

Passion for the name and reputation of God, a heart which grieves over what grieves God, and a passion for the advancement of the Kingdom require that we crucify ideas of comfort, safety, and security. However, it doesn't mean we are reckless or foolish in what we do. **We take calculated risks.** Paul and Jesus both fled areas where they knew their lives had been specifically targeted (they also had already delivered their messages there). Yet, they both intentionally entered areas they knew to be dangerous and hostile to their message. The risk was weighed against the task God had given them. They faithed their way through difficulties trusting in the Lord to orchestrate circumstances to His specifications for the task.

What must be understood is that often, risk is overestimated or inflated in our eyes. I remember while attending a wealthy church, God led me to start ministries to the disadvantaged in three local neighborhoods. Two of those areas were viewed as extremely dangerous by church members who wanted to work with me. They were fearful of property damage and physical safety if they even entered the areas. I told them to pray and trust in the Lord that He would protect them just as He protected those of His people who actually lived in these neighborhoods. They entered the areas in fear and trembling and found out that things were not as dangerous as they thought. They had gotten their perceptions of the area from mass media. All they had ever heard were the reports of crime sensationalized through print, image or voice media. In all the time we worked in these communities, not one robbery, act of vandalism or physical assault ever took place.

It is essential that we be "wise as serpents but harmless as doves." It is also essential that we not be controlled by our fears and apprehensions. Ultimately we must confront false ideas about how God wants us to live in the world. He has made it clear that if salt loses its saltiness it is only good for paving material. If light is placed under a bushel (nice safe place), it defeats its purpose for existence. We have been saved for the purpose of good works, extending the influence and presence of God and His Kingdom in the world. The Kingdom of God is extended by force and forceful people advance it (Matthew 11:12).

In one particular instance a family challenged me and stated that they didn't think God would ask them to put their family in a potentially dangerous situation. My reply was that if God did not spare His own Son to accomplish redemption and to reclaim the Kingdom, what makes them think that He would spare them? Are they greater than Jesus? Did they think they would be safe by disobeying God?

The issue of faithing life exposes what we really believe about God and where the affections of our hearts actually lie. Do we see God as being some weak, ineffectual, incompetent, senile old man? Do we believe evil is so strong that God can't counter it? Is He unable to care for us? Is His arm shortened that it cannot save? Or, are we so overwhelmed and awed by the greatness, the power, the wisdom of God that we are bold enough to tackle problems which are worthy of Him? He has assured us that the gates of Hell will not prevail against our onslaughts (Matthew 16:18). He has bound Himself to promises assuring action when His followers obediently engage the world attempting to overturn the works of the devil. Shake off the fear and allow the Spirit to energize you. Step out into the certainty of faithing.

Be ambitious in the Kingdom

Together you and your family members will decide the steps of faithing you will take to release control of your **time, treasure and talents** into the sovereign hands of God. The value of your actions will be made evident in the level of sacrifice involved. After all, you are participating in worship when you act in this manner (Romans 12:1-2). Remember the lessons from the book of Malachi... sacrifices to God must be the best, not the left over. Be bold in your choices, challenge yourself so that success will be determined by God's strength not yours. Surplus time and surplus money don't impress God. The test is how costly is the sacrifice, for that reveals the true state of the heart of the one making the sacrifice.

*Therefore, since we are surrounded by such a great cloud of witnesses, **let us throw off everything that*** *hinders and the sin that so easily entangles, and let us run with perseverance the race marked out for us. Let us fix our eyes on Jesus, the author and perfecter of our faith, who for the joy set before him endured the cross, scorning its shame, and sat down at the right hand of the throne of God. Consider him who endured such opposition from sinful men, so that you will not grow weary and lose heart. In your struggle against sin, you have not yet resisted to the point of shedding your blood. Heb. 12:1ff*

God has made us for such action. He made us in His image. He placed within us creativity and imagination which when yielded to His influence can enable us to dream amazing solutions to difficult problems besetting our communities. It is time to allow God to energize our dreams and begin faithing new futures for our families in the generations to come. I pray for my grandchildren's grandchildren, who they will marry, what they will do with their lives. I then live my life now in a manner which will present the reality of the risen Christ to my grandchildren.

Summary

Allow your imagination to be stirred by the scriptures. Allow God to grow your perception of Him. He is much more than we can imagine, and if this is so, we should be living in a manner that shows we understand the immensity of His power and knowledge and attempt tasks which reveal our willingness to trust Him.

It takes faithing to willingly limit our lifestyles so that we make room for God to live through us. It takes faithing to abandon the American Dream and embrace God's Kingdom agenda. It takes faithing to pursue downward mobility in how we spend our money, freeing up resources to support missionaries, aid the poor and needy, fund medical care, and advance the Kingdom in countless other ways. It takes faithing to open your life to the inconveniences, interruptions and challenges which will enter your life once you make yourself available to God. It takes faithing to willingly take upon you the sufferings of others in order to help them endure and introduce them to God.

Without faithing, it is impossible to please God.

*I just got home from working at **Mustard Seeds and Mountains**. This was an unforgettable experience. **It has definitely inspired me to do something in my own home town.** Autumn Young, OH*

*I got back from working at **Mustard Seeds and Mountains** and I loved it! Great experience, wouldn't trade it for anything. God really spoke to me. Emilee, MI*

It definitely showed me that I can make a difference. *It's amazing that when you stop and take a look around, you see needy people. People need help, need love, need Jesus. And we can give them those things. Why don't we? **We need to be living these things out. We need to make missions our life.** David, FL*

Chapter 7

Helping your family live out Kingdom values

I think we can agree that nothing shapes and solidifies family values like putting the teachings of the scriptures to work in the real world. When families join together in a common task advancing the Kingdom of God, they open themselves to new and powerful learning opportunities in which the reality and relevance of the gospel is brought to the forefront as it affects them personally and as they see the impact of the service in others' lives and the community.

In the same way, serving together brings with it the opportunity for the regard and respect of family members for one another to increase as they see how God uses them in trying circumstances. Too often children and parents suffer from nearsightedness in relation to the true gifts, strengths, abilities and character of each other. Parents tend to take children too lightly, overlooking abilities and gifts they possess and consequently lowering their expectations and failing to provide challenges worthy of their potential. Children tend to focus on parental flaws and inconsistencies, often in trivial areas, discounting the wisdom and capabilities of the parents. This is often due to context. The realm of the family is the family…a narrow context in which roles and expectations are clearly defined. Life settles into routines. These routines, in their predictability, tend to reinforce specific ways of interaction and attitudes between family members. The context of home is hopefully safe, supportive and nurturing. What happens when the context is altered? We all know the power of moving people from their "comfort zones".

Stepping out of your comfort zone

One thing family service does is alter the context in which family members view one another. When a family leaves the comfort of their home, when their routines are altered, when they encounter myriads of challenges, the potential for learning and personal transformation increases considerably. I have a friend, Keith Wasserman, who states, *Perspective is everything, everything.* Keith runs a homeless shelter in Ohio. In order not to lose perspective, Keith has chosen at various times to become homeless in a strange city for a week. He lives on the street with little money and visits the same shelters and soup kitchens in the city. By doing this he sees the work he does from the perspective of those he serves. It has vastly changed how he goes about his work.

When families serve in their local community or on short-term mission trips, the change in context creates unpredictable teaching moments. Values are challenged, biases and prejudices are unmasked, latent fears are brought into the light, and assumptions about the world and how it works are brought into question. Stepping out of "our world" and into another context, when done with an open mind and heart, can be one of the most educational and life altering activities. We all tend to congregate around people just like us socio-economically, racially, or politically. We allow our values to be shaped by this reference group. We form assumptions about other groups based upon how our group views the way the world should be and how people in it should act. Our views of those outside our group are often caricatures or stereotypes based upon superficial observations. However, when we enter another's world with an open heart, sensitive to the Holy Spirit, we find that our assumptions and judgments have often been harsh and wrongheaded. Context shapes all of us. Understanding different contexts not only broadens our mind and understanding, it should also soften our hearts and inform our actions.

Discovering Jesus in a strange disguise

Mother Teresa would challenge people to encounter Jesus in a strange disguise when working among the poor. She understood that every aspect of how we live our lives has spiritual implications and consequences. In the New Testament, the post-resurrection accounts of Jesus often have people failing to recognize Him. In at least one instance, He keeps people from recognizing Him. The scriptures say...

Blessed are the pure in heart, for they will see God. Matt. 5:8

Whether or not we see Him depends on the condition of our heart. If our hearts are pure, completely committed to Christ, we will see Him where others do not. Even then, He may put us through a test to see where our hearts' allegiances lie, withholding His identity till a later date.

For I was hungry and you gave me something to eat, I was thirsty and you gave me something to drink, I was a stranger and you invited me in, I needed clothes and you clothed me, I was sick and you looked after me, I was in prison and you came to visit me.' *"Then the righteous will answer him, **'Lord, when did we see you hungry and feed you, or thirsty and***

give you something to drink? *When did we see you
a stranger and invite you in, or needing clothes and
clothe you? When did we see you sick or in prison
and go to visit you?' "The King will reply, 'I tell
you the truth,* **whatever you did for one of the least
of these brothers of mine, you did for me.'** *Matt.
25:35ff (emphasis mine)*

The habits we form in our lifestyle impact eternity.
Mother Teresa understood that Jesus seeks to interact with
us in ways which often don't fit our religious expectations
or tidy religious structures. Jesus chooses to encounter us
in the nitty gritty of life and often in the form of tests to our
commitment to Him by putting before us opportunities to
minister to Him.

By extending ourselves to the poor, to widows, to the
fatherless and to immigrants, we not only provide a social
service to the needy, we also provide a service to ourselves.
Our action helps to break down barriers of prejudice and
indifference in us. Our service softens our hearts and disman-
tles the cynicism which our culture constructs as a defense
to problems it doesn't understand or which seem resistant to
change. Our obedience and loving service demolishes argu-
ments and hostility within our culture toward Christ as His
love is brought to bear in concrete ways; unassailable proof
of His love and goodness to a skeptical world.

So, a very real first step in putting your faith into action
involves getting yourselves spiritually fit and ready for what
you may encounter. The work you will do will be spiritual
in nature, even if you are washing dishes. That's because the
work is a vehicle for ministry, just as the water pipes in your
house are a vehicle for delivering water. Your service provides opportunity for *redemptive relationships*. These are
relationships in which others are either brought to the point
of being followers of Christ or nurtured in their life with

Christ. This can take place within the family and most certainly is expected with anyone whom family members come into contact.

How to prepare the family for service

How do you prepare your family spiritually?

Learning precedes everything. Some advance preparation of the mind and heart is essential. Having regular family discussions regarding the Kingdom of God and its demands on our lives is a good first step in getting everyone on the same page. Next, having an understanding of the need for a sensitivity to and dependence on the Holy Spirit, the need for confession and repentance from sin, and a good understanding and ability to share the Gospel seems foundational.

Spiritual Preparation
- *Begin to study the Kingdom of God.*
- *Practice conversational sharing of your faith.*
- *Pray together on a regular basis for each other and God's direction in how your family is to serve.*
- *Read Henri Nouwen's book Compassion.*
- *Discuss what the Bible says about servanthood.*
- *Read the scriptures daily*
- *Discuss what it means to be sensitive to the Holy Spirit*

Many people are often intimidated and sometimes a little scared when they think of actually introducing someone to Christ. Explaining what it means to be a follower of Jesus and how essential the death, burial and resurrection of Jesus is to being a follower is foundational.

There are numerous books that deal with sharing your faith available. Some of the best deal with conversational evangelism, the art of using casual conversation as a means to share essential facts about God. Some great books to help you and your family to become proficient with this technique are, *Conversational Evangelism: How to Listen and Speak So You Can Be Heard* by Norman Geisler and David Geisler, or *Reimagining Evangelism: Inviting Friends on a Spiritual Journey* by Rick Richardson. Including a systematic study of one of these would be good preparation for your time of service.

Next, it would be good to look over the passages in scripture which talk about servanthood and humility. These two are linked and form the framework from which you will serve. When you understand and embrace the role of a servant, you free yourself to fully appreciate the significance of work you will encounter, no matter how mundane. You transform activities by your attitude. Your attitude of humility also opens you to greater understanding of the people you serve as well as the constraints the agency you serve with must overcome. Humble servants get past the tendency we all have to critique, judge and second guess others.

Having a general understanding of these issues is enough for beginning. Don't feel that all must stop until you master all of these areas of study. You and your family can learn as you go. In fact, your service may highlight how necessary these studies are and become the prime motivator for pursuing them.

What does it mean to be a servant and not a sergeant?

You can serve without being a servant but you can't be a servant without serving. It's important that you enter into your relationship with the ministry you select with an open mind and a heart ready to do anything they ask you to do. Chances are what they ask you to do will be mundane, grunt type work. That doesn't mean the work is meaningless or unneeded. In all likelihood it will be greatly needed and because you are doing it, more qualified staff are freed to deal more directly with their clients, or freed to tackle higher level problems.

You may be thinking, *"I want more direct involvement with the public. I want to be more involved in service delivery. I want to see their faces."* This is important and yet may not always be feasible. Why? Although you are volunteering and are seeking an activity to challenge your family, the achievement of your goals is not the first concern of the ministry you are serving. The ministry is concerned with meeting the needs of the people they serve in a manner that affirms their dignity, builds them up, and points them to Christ. That may mean that the person served is best ministered to by someone who has already established a trusting relationship with them. Bringing a stranger into the picture can break trust and create feelings of inferiority, injuring the person's dignity.

We often get people in our ministry who want to come in during holidays and hand out gifts to kids in the area. They genuinely want to help brighten these kids' lives. They are adamant that they want to be the ones who hand out the gifts. We inform them that although they are interested in getting a great feeling from helping others in this manner, it isn't the primary goal of our organization to make them feel good. We are more interested in the long term effects on the local people we serve. We help outsiders see that often, when strangers come in to shower gifts on children, the parents of the children are embarrassed and ashamed that they are unable to provide similar things for their children. In addition, we point out that when people are merely given things, their sense of responsibility and dignity is damaged (for an in depth study of this look at the book mentioned earlier, *When helping hurts*). We then tell the potential volunteers that we feel it is best to make the gifts available to the parents either through a voucher program or through a small fee for the gift. The parent then feels empowered from having been able to purchase, even at a much discounted price, gifts which they can give to their own children. The parent rather than a stranger gets the gratitude and love of the child. Can you see how important this is?

The scriptures also teach that those who do the background work are just as responsible for the results as those who do the upfront work. The key concept to embrace is that although you are helping out at a particular ministry, you are actually doing the work to, for and with Jesus.

> *What, after all, is Apollos? And what is Paul? Only servants, through whom you came to believe-as the Lord has assigned to each his task.* ***I planted the seed, Apollos watered*** *it, but* ***God made it grow.*** *So neither he who plants nor he who waters is anything, but only God, who makes things grow.* ***The man who plants and the man who waters have one purpose, and each will be rewarded according to his own labor.*** *For we are God's fellow workers; you are God's field, God's building. 1 Cor. 3:5 (emphasis mine)*

In addition, the scriptures are clear that it is important to prove a person before putting them in places of authority. The upfront work may not be possible until you are proven to be dependable, sensitive and exhibiting Christ-like characteristics.

One of the first things to remember is that you and your family are there to serve, not to critique or offer advice on how better to do the job. Unless you have been working with the ministry for quite some time and had time to reflect upon their strategy and tactics, you probably have insufficient knowledge of the constraints and pressures associated with what they are trying to do to make useful recommendations.

Remember, you are in a learning/serving mode. Open yourself up to the joy of being surprised. Suspend judgment and the need for control. Look at the world with new eyes. What may appear to be inefficient is really highly effective. What may appear to be a waste of time is more of an investment in people. Allow yourself time to learn what you don't know you don't know.

How to be the best servant you can be

There are tremendous amounts of literature, film and conferences related to the responsibilities of leaders and the characteristics of good leadership. Only recently has there been serious attention given to the traits and responsibilities of good followership. Research shows that the best leaders are powerless in the face of followers who refuse to cooperate or meet the leader's high expectations. What are the characteristics of a good servant, in biblical terms?

Good servants assume responsibility

Good servants assume responsibility for how they affect the outcomes and reputation of the organization they serve. By doing this, a sense of community is fostered in the organization while the synergistic power of multiple checks and balances takes place. Too often individuals take an hourly employee mentality that leads to only doing what one is told and an avoidance of taking initiative. A good servant looks for ways to improve the activities and reputation of the organization, becoming a partner with the leader.

The first step in this process involves taking responsibility for yourself. Good servants monitor and assess their own actions, striving for excellence in job performance, personal attitude and speech. Is the servant doing the best possible work and anticipating problems or challenges? Is the servant striving to improve his or her skills and knowledge of the tasks at hand, seeking to become the best in his or particular task? Is the servant aware of his or her particular weaknesses and creating learning and practice plans to overcome them? Taking personal action involves recognizing that it is your personal responsibility to assess and monitor yourself. This acknowledges that those who have responsibility for supervising you are not super humans who intuitively know everything. The servant is a partner with the leader in their development. Failure to take responsibility here could not only hurt the servant, but the organization. Have you ever been around followers who spoke in a demeaning manner toward leaders, used body language that communicated rebellion or dissatisfaction, participated in gossip or complaining about tasks or relationships? If so, you have experienced firsthand the impact failing to assume responsibility for one's own actions and attitudes can have in an organization.

Next, be aware of the style of learning and following you exhibit. Think of your work style. Do you need a lot of supervisory support in tasks? Does it differ in high or low challenge situations? Do you feel like you have been abandoned if you don't receive feedback often? Do you feel like you are micromanaged when supervisors check in too often? Knowing these issues and communicating them to leaders in the organization, and adjusting expectations will help you not only be more productive and satisfied, but help create a more pleasant work environment.

Elicit feedback from others to gain better perspective on your work. Good servants overcome their aversion and oversensitivity to criticism. Because they want to become all God has in store for them, they are aware that they have "blind spots" in their lives and need others' perspectives in order for these blind areas to come to light. Being open to instruction is one of the first characteristics of wisdom that comes from God (James 3:13ff). Having an open and supportive environment helps facilitate excellence and deep communication. Eliminating defensiveness and blaming is essential. By being self-critical in a positive way, we become open to suggestions of others. This leads to open and trusting communication since each person realizes that no one is out to personally harm them.

Remember, the feedback you get may not be negative or of a critical nature. You may well find yourself being praised for work done and godly traits being developed in you. This will do much to bolster a sense of self-efficacy and esteem and counter the attacks of the evil one (the great accuser).

Personal growth is a prime goal of good servants. God has entrusted to each person talents and abilities that He intends we develop to the fullest extent. For personal growth to take place, we must be courageous enough to be ruthlessly honest with ourselves. We must have a clear view of our strengths as well as our limitations and our weaknesses. There is no room for personal deception that either falsely puffs up or falsely downplays our strengths or weaknesses. Challenge will be at the heart of growth and good servants are open to new challenges and learning new skills.

Practice self-management (taking care of ourselves). Good servants learn how to organize their lives and structure their work and environment. Good self-management reveals itself in timeliness (not only being on time but completing work in a timely manner), being prepared for tasks or meetings (doing the necessary homework, anticipating needs before they arise), forward thinking (the ability to plan out tasks and anticipate challenges), and stewardship (the frugal use of resources, time and activity). Self-managers not only look after job related tasks but personal tasks such as getting enough rest, exercise, nutrition, spiritual development, and intellectual and social stimulation.

Fuel your passion and develop a love for your work. Any task whether mundane, boring, odious or difficult can be transformed into worship. The passion lies in the heart and its relationship to the Lord, not in the task. Brother Lawrence, in the little book *Practicing the Presence of God*, points out that even washing dishes can be a divine appointment and source of joy. Learn to frame the current task in the bigger picture of how God is using it to accomplish larger goals. Be alert to emotions like frustration, complaint, dissatisfaction, and aversion. When these arise, look to their source and purpose to rise above feelings. In some instances, your dissatisfaction may point to larger organizational needs such as altering strategy, tactics or vision. Be open to sharing those with leadership and also open to the input from leaders which may run counter to your solutions.

Develop initiative. The willingness to initiate action without instruction is a sign of maturity and commitment to organizational goals and values. Find out ahead of time the boundaries the organization has on your ability to make decisions. You may be surprised to discover you have more authority and power than you realized. When you are confronted with challenges, problems, or tasks that you are well-equipped to handle personally, as well as within your sphere of authority in the organization, and you fail to act, you not only impoverish the organization and community, you injure yourself. Your inaction erodes the development of personal responsibility and reinforces values that diminish your reputation in the organization.

Having the courage to represent the leader is foundational to service as well. This may involve defending the leader's actions to those within or outside the organization. Leaders often face opposition within and without the organization. Too often, insufficient information, rumor or conjecture is circulated by this opposition causing the leader's actions, motives or intentions to be misrepresented or misunderstood. Good servants recognize this and not only refuse to be part of the circuit of disinformation, but actively defend and clarify what is really happening. It is not that the servant ignores legitimate concerns or criticisms; it is that the servant is committed to the concerns and criticisms being handled correctly, in a manner that will lead to resolution while maintaining the fragile nature of community and mutual support each member of the organization has labored so diligently to create.

Since the general public does not have the opportunity to have access to the leader at the same level as the servant, the servant helps to define the leader and leader's actions to the public. The servant's goal is for the leader to succeed. Therefore, the servant seeks to magnify the leader's positive qualities while providing service to enrich those areas where the leader is weak.

Good servants participate in transformation.

Modeling change is the single most effective method for affecting leader behavior. As the old saying goes, *"If you want to change the world, begin with yourself"*. Focusing only on the leader can cause the servant to become manipulative. By focusing on ourselves, we place our attention on the one area where we have ultimate power to bring about change. Servants can look to their own behavior to see if they have attitudes, responses or reactions that reinforce negative or destructive leader behaviors. Do we look the other way when the leader embarks on a course of action that may not be illegal but is certainly unethical? The servant's failure to challenge the leader reinforces the leader's aberrant behavior.

Servants can help leaders become aware of difficulties within their leadership style or direction before they escalate into crisis conditions. The key is for the servant to find ways to alert the leader without making the leader defensive and still convey the servant's support and respect for the leader. It is important to differentiate the leader from the leader's behavior.

A troubling reality is that often the servant is no more perfect than the leader. Both leader and servant have strengths and weaknesses. The servant can facilitate willingness to change in the leader by being open and vulnerable with the leader regarding his own strengths and weaknesses and willingness to change. By modeling openness to change ourselves, we create an arena for dialogue in a supportive, non-threatening environment. As threatened as the servant sometimes feels in the presence of the leader, it is important for the servant to realize that the leader is also sensitive to the climate generated by the servants. Having openness to transformation, modeling vulnerability, modeling change and communicating support and acceptance allow leaders to be vulnerable and open without fear of negative repercussions.

How do you prepare for the cross-cultural experience?

I encourage people to become budding experts on the areas where they intend to serve. Are you going to work with the homeless? Learn about homelessness in your area. How many are there? What are the primary reasons for their homelessness? Pick up some books that deal with homelessness, especially some written from the perspective of being homeless, and read them together, discussing them. I encourage people to look at poverty in general and begin to grasp the challenges, tensions and traps associated with poverty both in the United States and abroad. Ruby Paine's book, *A Framework for understanding poverty* provides great insight into poverty in the U.S. Viv Grigg's books, *Companion to the poor* and *Cry of the urban poor* are great for getting the feel for poverty in the 2/3 world. Another great book for understanding how you should approach the poverty you encounter is *When helping hurts: How to alleviate poverty without hurting the poor or yourself*, by Fikkert and Corbett.

Cross-cultural Preparation

- *Learn about poverty*
- *Research the culture or area where you intend to serve*
- *Watch movies which help you understand how cultural misunderstandings take place*
- *Find out about culture shock, what causes it and what you can do about it.*
- *Look at the history of the people or area where you are going.*

If you are going to another culture, learn as much as you can about that culture and their practices and traditions. Saturate your mind with their history; their current status economically, socially, politically, racially etc.; their myths or religious practices; their relationship with cultures around them; significant events or people in their history. Maybe you can learn some basic phrases in their language in order to greet them, ask basic questions, etc.

You also need to sensitize yourself to your own tendency to judge the world through the filter of your culture. There are cultural games like *Bafa Bafa, Luna* or *Bargna*. These are simulation games that help you feel and experience being misunderstood or misjudged. Bargna is a card game that helps you see how different perspectives and expectations in a simple game can lead to misunderstanding, judgmental attitudes and hurt feelings. If this can happen in a game, how much more probable is this in real life where the rules aren't known? Bafa Bafa (sometimes called Luna) actually makes you a representative of a culture and responsible for communicating your values to other cultures. You end up realizing that how you live in and make sense of the world is not how others live in and make sense of the world. These are fun and quickly point out that common sense is only common in your culture.

There are fun movies the family can watch which portray the misunderstandings which can arise cross-culturally. *My Big Fat Greek Wedding* is not only funny, but points out various ways we misunderstand other cultures. *The Gods Must Be Crazy* highlights how a seemingly innocuous addition to the technology of a tribe adversely affects their life. *Finding Forrester* provides insight into class and racial differences and our tendency to stereotype and prejudge. There are many others. *The Blind Side* is a true story of a family taking in a homeless youth and how it altered his future. *Slumdog Millionaire* is a troubling movie that gives insight into slum children in India. Each provide numerous teaching moments. Watch them ahead of time to discover where the movie can be stopped and a discussion started about what is happening.

Remember that even with all you learn through reading, watching film, or participating in simulations, etc., once you land on the ground in that new context, you are as ignorant as a small child in terms of the deep meanings and assumptions that shape behavior in that setting. You must move from "banking learning", where you study material ahead of time and store away information, to experiential learning, where you must draw on experience and knowledge, and utilize keen observation to learn how to function well. Experiential learning requires that you be sensitive to the Holy Spirit, relying upon Him to draw your attention to important practices and reactions of people around you. You will enter the realm of *action and reflection*. People only learn from their experience *if* they learn from their experience. To learn you must reflect on interactions, analyze situations, act based upon your new knowledge and then enter a time of reflection again as you deal with responses from people and the environment. You will have to slow down, take more time. This type of learning requires much deeper processing than banking learning. This type of learning continues for as long as you expose yourself to the environment.

I have been in ministry in West Virginia over 16 years now, and I am still learning new things which alter my perceptions of the people and how they live their lives. This new knowledge forces me to change approaches and strategies. The same will be true for you. The tendency initially, especially if you have been diligent in learning about the area and people where you serve, is to think that you know more than you do. You fail to see how superficial your knowledge really is. You draw from your store of wisdom, developed in another context, and try to apply it to the new context. Most often you will find that your ideas fall flat because they fail to address real values or expectations which are not in your context but present in this cultural setting. Being willing and able to let go and become a learner rather than a teacher is a crucial step in really being effective in your service.

You will use this act/reflect process throughout your service activities in order to process information about the environment and the people and the effectiveness of your interaction with them. You will also use this process to make sense of the spiritual impact your service is having upon you and family members. Engaging in action/reflection enables you to isolate recurring themes of challenge or spiritual warfare and know better how to counter them. It also enables you to develop insight into your own spiritual condition. Again, patterns of temptation, failure, discouragement, and frustration, as well as insights into spiritual giftedness, areas of individual interest, how family members interact together, strengths of individuals and how these combine to form a portrait of family strengths become evident when being forced to take a new perspective through reflecting on these various levels of life and roles.

Choosing a place to serve

How is God moving in your family?

The first consideration for you and your family is how God seems to be working in your hearts individually and collectively. Has He placed a concern or burden on one or more of your family members for a particular people (widows, orphans, homeless, handicapped), social issue (human trafficking, children soldiers, poverty, refugees) or religious focus (planting churches, frontier missions, reaching unreached people)? Discerning how He may be leading you as a family is important. If there is no clear leading, you may target one of the above groups or issues mentioned for an exploratory experience.

> *Our youngest son was more quiet and reserved than our older son and not as prone to athletics. He tended to be more artistic. We had decided to work with a local ministry that had started a prep school in the inner city. While our oldest son played games and led studies, our youngest designed a leather medallion and worked with kids to burn the image with a wood burning tool onto a leather disk and color it with water colors. The kids in the school loved it and our son beamed with joy.*

Next, how has God gifted you as a family? Do you have particular skills or abilities you can offer to an organization? Are all of you able to share these skills or abilities? As I have mentioned in chapter 1, God has uniquely gifted each family member and these gifts can be brought to bear. However, there is a caution with this. **Your possession or lack of particular gifts should not be the primary factors in choosing where to serve**. Often, missionaries find themselves serving in areas where they are not gifted because the work just needs to be done. God then comes and empowers them to do what is necessary. In the same manner, you may find that you are asked to take on tasks you have never before encountered. When this happens, you will get the joy of seeing how God can take your readiness and willingness to serve and use you to do something you never would have thought you could do. His power will work through you.

Ask, Seek, Knock. This is a three-pronged process Jesus outlined in prayer.

> *"**Ask** and it will be given to you; **seek** and you will find; **knock** and the door will be opened to you. For everyone who asks receives; he who seeks finds; and to him who knocks, the door will be opened. Matt. 7 (emphasis mine)*

Prayer for many people is a passive activity. For some, it's merely a means to calming frayed emotions, sort of like whistling as you walk past a graveyard. Many link the idea of passively waiting to prayer. I pray, and then I wait. If nothing happens, then it isn't God's will (a fatalist approach at best). Jesus proposes an activist approach to prayer. **Go to the Father and ask**, tell Him your concerns, desires, fears, etc. **Then, begin to seek.** This involves active investigation of options, solutions, and possible courses of action. We employ seeking in nearly every aspect of our lives on a daily basis. Where can we get the best price on car repairs and still have them done well? Where can we get the best medical treatment and still have our insurance apply? What is the best type of mountain bike to purchase for the type of riding I do? All these highlight seeking. Why is it that when it comes to identifying God's direction in our lives, we suddenly become passive, asking for direction but passively waiting for answers to fall from the sky? Jesus presses for action. I was told as a young follower of Christ that you can only steer a moving ship. Look through scripture: God tends to select people who are doing something to accomplish His tasks. Their activity, their seeking of Him enabled Him to guide them.

The final part of the process is **knocking**. This means getting out and pounding on doors, examining and exploring potential areas of ministry. God will open and close the doors He sees fit.

> *I know your deeds. See,* ***I have placed before you an open door*** *that no one can shut. ... Rev. 3:8*

This stage places you on the ground in the community. You begin to experience with your senses where you might serve. Your conversations with people will give you insight into the organization and the local culture. Your visits will do more to inform you of context, potential fit with the work or the organization than nearly anything else you could do. Your movement in the community, your active seeking, your careful investigation, are all used by the Holy Spirit to influence your mind and heart. His direction comes as you move about, proving that you are ready to do His will. Too many people passively pray for God to reveal to them His will and yet have no intention of ever doing what is revealed. Those who are actively seeking and knocking are those most likely to obey the King.

Local or short-term mission trip?

At first this seems like an easy question to answer. Local is closer and you would think that local involvement would be easier to engage in. In some ways this is true. However, what we have found is that going on a short-term mission trip as a family to an area outside your local environment is a more powerful way to ignite mission vision as well as launch your involvement locally. This is true for a number of reasons.

First, having to leave your comfortable home, your predictable schedules and patterns of living, leaving behind friends, leaving behind modern technology and entering into a much more simple form of life and schedule has a greater impact on family members. You are in unfamiliar territory and old patterns of interaction, old rote modes of dealing with the world are out the window. Being off balance in a strange environment creates an attentiveness and energy that can't be duplicated locally.

Next, the impact of culture and the inability to escape it forces family members to critically look at their own culture and lifestyle. Immersion in language is the best way to learn a language. Immersion in culture is the best way to open our eyes to our own ethnocentrism and prejudices. This is especially true when a mentor is present who can help force family members to move beyond superficial observations regarding the culture to more substantial issues of worldview and values.

Third, it is often easier to serve in another culture because of anonymity. You have greater freedom to make mistakes, engage in public activity, and even undertake risky activity in another culture than in your own. After all, you will leave at the end of a period of time and return to your own area. When you are at home, people you know see you; your reputation is at stake. Also, in your local culture, you are forced to face prejudices, attitudes and assumptions about various groups you may encounter locally. Your attitudes about local ethnicities, religions, races, or social classes harass you more at home since that is where your opinions and values were formed. Going to another culture places you in a different context and you may not have to confront those same attitudes or values which are contrary to scripture. In another culture, as an observer, you hear of and see their attitudes toward different groups, their tendencies to prejudge and discriminate and begin to understand how damaging this can be in society. Since their focal groups are different from the ones you find difficult at home, you are less defensive when confronted with teaching on the need for reconciliation, forgiveness and the need to cross cultural, social, class, status and racial barriers in order to bring about understanding, acceptance, and appreciation of others. Often you are forced to address your own attitudes toward other groups at home. Because the animosity toward cultural groups and issues are different in another culture, it seems safer psychologically to address the need for reconciliation, and therefore you are more open to new values.

Fourth, trips to assist agencies in other cultures may be easier because the agencies may be structured for handling volunteers more than groups around your home. After all, if they are bringing in volunteers from the outside, they should be ready to mentor them. (You would think this to be true, but too often it isn't. Later we will look at how to choose the best agency for service.) Local agencies, especially smaller ones, may be so inundated with work that they have not completely thought through how best to handle volunteers. They are still worthy for service, you just have to adjust your expectations as to the kind of support and teaching they can provide for you and your family.

How do you pick an organization?

Since you are reading this book, I assume that you are interested in working with faith-based agencies as opposed to working with secular, social agencies. I am not opposed to working with secular groups and have worked with them myself as a volunteer in the past. I believe in being "yeasty", permeating every strata of society with the presence of followers of Jesus. Serving in a secular organization doubles the potential for witnessing about Christ by including the staff of the organization as well. However, should you decide to move in that direction you should be prepared to deal with the restrictions they will place on your ability to share about your life with Christ. Many secular organizations will actually require you to be silent about your relationship with Jesus, whether dealing with staff or clients. A very few may even be hostile toward you because you seek to allow Christ to permeate every aspect of your life. Welcome to the age of intolerance in the name of tolerance.

My perspective is that true, transformational change involves major value and worldview changes. Values are anchored in spiritual assumptions about the world and your place in it. For this reason, being able to address the spiritual aspect of life is essential to long-term transformational change. Even in Alcoholics Anonymous it is recognized that it is essential to involve the spiritual for lasting change (they call it a higher power). Consequently, I recommend that you identify faith-based organizations for short-term mission trips and local service. Focusing on faith-based groups will ensure that you deal holistically with those you serve and you will help advance the Kingdom God.

Short-term trips

Putting short-term mission trips into perspective

The idea of going on a short-term mission trip is both exciting and somewhat scary. This is especially true if you are experiencing a short-term trip for the first time. There are some key things to remember. First short-term mission trips are the launching pad, not the destination. Short-term trips serve numerous purposes but should not be placed on some pedestal that turns them into some type of hyper-spiritual activity. Chances are you will get on a spiritual high while on your trip. It will be a highlight of your year's spiritual growth. The trip serves to further your commitment and understanding of mission and to solidify your family's commitment to *Mission as Life*. It is an opportunity for your family members to put their gifts to work in an unfamiliar environment and to celebrate how God uniquely uses each family member.

Second, short-term trips act as a catalyst for spiritual growth. The pressures and demands either from daily living conditions, specific ministry tasks, or family dynamics bring to light areas of spiritual strength and weakness for each person. Consequently, it is important that everyone go into the trip with a strong commitment to extend grace and understanding to one another. You really can't go wrong when you seek to maintain the unity of the Spirit to create a bond of peace. Sometimes on short-term trips people encounter situations that shake them to their foundations. They can have powerful emotional responses to needs in the people they serve as well as powerful emotional responses to things which God is dealing with in their lives. Nerves become frayed and people can lose perspective. Knowing from the outset that the trip is not the pinnacle of spiritual growth but rather the base of the mountain or a base camp somewhere on the mountain helps people realize that what they are encountering is part of a longer growth process. They need to understand they will learn some things on the trip, but the deeper processing and learning takes place after the trip.

I see short-term trips as a type of spiritual retreat. A time to recalibrate one's inner compass to correspond with God's will. When taken with the right agency, they can ignite a vision for missions and inspire family members to make truly life changing decisions in how they invest their time, treasure, and talents.

Literally millions of people each year participate in short-term mission trips. All types of trips are available, yet most focus on either youth or adult teams. Few agencies truly focus on family-oriented trips. This should be of primary importance when looking at selecting an agency for a short-term trip. In addition, there are a number of other key factors, a) is the agency locally centered or does it travel in and leave after a season; b) is the agency holistic in its approach; c) does the agency provide mentoring by seasoned missionary staff; d) are materials provided for pre-training and post-trip follow through; e) does the agency provide cultural sensitivity training; f) is the work suitable for all family members; g) and does the agency provide guidance for long-term implementation of a mission lifestyle? Granted, these are all hefty issues expected from each agency, yet, if your short-term trip is to go beyond a mere "Christian tourism" and become a launching pad or key event in your *Mission as Life* journey, these elements should be present.

Choosing an organization in which to serve
- *Is the agency locally based?*
- *Is the agency holistic in its approach?*
- *Does the agency provide seasoned mentors?*
- *Are there materials for pre-training and post-trip follow through?*
- *Does the agency provide cultural sensitivity training?*
- *Can the agency provide work suitable for the family?*
- *Does the agency provide guidance in promoting a mission as life lifestyle?*

There are a number of agencies which book teams for work trips or mission trips and who do not have permanent presence in the communities in which they serve. They've chosen to do this for a number of reasons. I don't intend to launch a full discussion on the pros and cons of this practice; that would require nearly another book. My bias is toward locally based agencies because research has shown that they have greater long-term, lasting impact on the area served. These are agencies that have chosen to move into a community and invest time and resources in transforming that community.

When an agency is locally based, they participate in the life of the community. They become familiar, as an insider, with the tensions, the hopes, the frustrations and the dreams of that community. They are tuned into what makes the local people and community "tick". By living among the people, interacting with them in numerous settings, suffering with them through challenges, they gain invaluable insight into their worldview and aspirations. The future of the agency is linked to the community. The people are more than acquaintances to them. They are their neighbors. The people are more than a means to minister to teams, they are the focus of the agency.

Some agencies seek to utilize local churches or agencies as brokers for them. The local groups act as consultants to the outside group in the type of work done and families selected. The problem with this is that ultimate control resides in the hands of the outside agency. You may also find that local people have not been given appropriate training responsibility and are unprepared, especially as it relates to spiritual and cultural training.

A locally based agency should also have the funds raised through it reinvested into the local community rather than having large portions shuttled to a main office in another area. The agency's primary focus should be the transformation of the local community.

Is the agency holistic in its approach

Look for agencies which deal with the whole person. As a follower of Christ, it is important that we are involved in the total transformation of people. This means that spiritual transformation is essential for breaking the old habits which enslave people in poverty, addiction, and self-destructive actions and cycles. (There are some 400+ agencies associated with the Christian Community Development Association and who emphasize holistic approaches to dealing with the marginalized.) Ask the agency where you want to serve how important evangelism is in their service opportunities. Many agencies function as social agencies and forgo any sharing of the gospel of Jesus Christ. To advance the Kingdom of God, one must proclaim the good news of Jesus Christ, His sacrificial death for our sin and His resurrection.

Does the agency provide seasoned mentors

It is important that the agency utilize seasoned, trained staff as primary teachers and mentors. Many agencies use college interns to oversee all aspects of their work, including spiritual and cultural training and counsel. Utilizing college staff for overseeing worksites is fine. However, having a spiritually mature teacher/mentor will be essential for making the most of your short-term trip. This person has much more insight into local culture and can help make sense of things you will encounter during your stay. A seasoned mentor will also be able to bring the scriptures to bear in a much more powerful and focused manner, drawing out challenges, insights, and nuances which relate not only to the culture in which you are working, but in relation to the challenges, questions and stresses you and your family are undergoing as you serve in that culture. A seasoned mentor can also help you through nightly debriefing and analysis of what happened that day and what you can learn from what you encountered. The mentor acts as a guide, forcing you and your family to address questions you didn't even know existed.

Materials for pre-training and post-trip follow through

The agency you select should provide ample materials for preparing for your trip. Do they provide devotionals for spiritual preparation before the trip? Are there materials which will guide you in what to do after the trip? Most volunteers find themselves overwhelmed with the trip itself. Too often volunteers fail to think beyond the trip or often, because of how they've been trained in their churches, fail to think outside the church box in terms of how they will apply their new knowledge and motivation to reach their community. Study materials and resources provided by the agency can help families make their intention to follow through at home a reality.

Having resources that you can use once the trip is over to deepen your understanding of the Kingdom of God is what takes your involvement from an event orientation to a lifestyle orientation. Ask them for these follow-up type studies or materials.

Cultural sensitivity training

What does the agency do to help you and your family adjust to the culture? Do they provide training which helps you and your family understand the local mindset? Do they provide training which helps you discover your prejudices and stereotypes? How will they help you grasp the nuances of the local culture? These questions will help you discover how well the agency is prepared to work with outside volunteers and how sensitive the agency is to their local culture. We make it a point to sensitize outsiders to the various ways local people can be offended. We also make it a point to help outsiders understand that their assumptions about how to live in the world may differ vastly from assumptions in our local culture. By providing this type of training, countless misunderstandings are avoided and the ability of the volunteering family to quickly begin to relate to local people accelerated.

Work suitable for the whole family

Many agencies structure work only for those who are 14 years of age or older. This presents a problem for families. Find out whether or not the agency makes accommodations for children in the way they select work for the family. Find out also if the agency tries to match up the skill level of the family with the type of work available.

When you contact the agency, be sure you inform them of any special needs your family has. For instance, because we are located in the Appalachian Mountains and most of our clientele are in substandard housing, it is difficult for us to fully accommodate those with physical limitations who want to volunteer. The steep terrain often coupled with multiple stairs to homes, or doorways that are only 27 inches wide, provide challenges. Still, we work diligently to match the work with person's ability. By letting us know ahead of time, we have more time to find just the right place.

Next, be reasonable about what you expect in relation to your children. It is obvious that if you have children under five, someone in the family will have to spend time watching your children. Their participation will be limited even though they will be soaking up the environment. Often, small children have the ability to teach adults about a much overlooked ministry, the ministry of being. Let me explain.

While my wife was undergoing breast cancer treatment, I damaged my left knee. I had already had a knee replacement on the right-side and now one was needed on the left. I knew what I was facing and I was a little depressed. The night before the surgery, my little 2 ½ year old grandson came to my room dressed in his Superman outfit. He wanted me to help him fly…as well as hum the superman flying song. We played together, he jabbered away in his own language, we looked at Superman pictures on the internet, and he flew, and flew, and flew. When he left I was feeling wonderful. He had taught me that just being with someone ministers powerfully to them. Your young children, especially when placed with the elderly, may have the same effect.

Children from the ages of five up have different capacities for work. The older they are, the more substantial the task they can undertake and the longer they can work. I have taken a team of 5th graders and given them the task of moving 20 tons of gravel to make a road. They all worked diligently all day and finished the job in 2 days. They and their parents were astounded and proud. They had a great time! With families, we often have them work half days and spend the rest of the day focusing on the Lord together or visiting with local people. This enables the younger or more distracted children to have variety and a break in which they can burn off energy and soak up local culture.

Provide guidance in the Mission as Life lifestyle

Research has shown that the majority of short-term trips are merely seen as special events by the participants and the agencies who conduct them. Few people and few agencies see them as a means to jumpstart a lifestyle built around radical Kingdom living or developing a lifestyle that turns mission service into a regular activity personally and in family life.

Does the agency you are looking at provide training in how to develop a *Mission as Life* lifestyle? On what does their teaching focus? Do their materials emphasize your returning to your own area and linking up with organizations there to serve your community? Do they try to facilitate your involvement locally? Do they have resources to which they can point you that will assist you in growing in your knowledge of having an activist perspective on the Kingdom of God?

At Mustard Seeds and Mountains we emphasize making ourselves available to come to churches and work with families to establish support networks of those who want to pursue this lifestyle. Having others who are seeking to embody Kingdom principles close by is important. You encourage one another, share ideas with one another, explore new service opportunities together, and share victories, challenges and stories.

Local agencies

Most of the criteria for short-term trips are applicable to local agencies as well, along with some exceptions. Serving locally should be the ultimate goal of you and your family since it allows you to integrate service into your lifestyle on a regular basis.

While those advertising short-term missions are clearly set up to handle volunteers, often local agencies, while utilizing volunteers, are sometimes not as fully prepared for volunteer involvement. Local agencies are more used to working with one or two people at a time who volunteer rather than large groups or whole families. While they may not have all the resources available that agencies who specialize in short-term trips must have, it doesn't necessarily mean they are not suitable for local family involvement. You may find that local agencies are much more flexible when it comes to family involvement than short-term agencies. You may also find that they provide greater "hands on" activity. What they lack in support materials they make up for in personal care and opportunity for more substantial involvement over time.

I recommend seeking out one or two agencies to work with rather than jumping around to multiple agencies. A key benefit of committing to only a few local agencies is your ability to see God work in the hearts and lives of the staff, clients, and your family members over time. Your long-term involvement with a work allows you to become one of the "insiders" in the minds of the staff and the clients served. I tell those who serve with us that because of their commitment, God will share with them His "secrets". These are insights gained through long-term relationships. Problems, hurts, failings, shortcomings; strengths, fruitful practices, and the image of God evident in people all are brought to your attention in the staff, clients and agencies in which you volunteer. God shares these in order to bring your gifts to bear in addressing them, burden your heart for prayer, and soften your heart as you see God at work in the lives of all involved. You realize that each person and each ministry is a work in progress, full of amazing evidence of God's work, as well as full of many areas where God needs to work. You and your family are also in process. Both you and the ministry with which you serve encounter each others strengths and weaknesses, amazing gifts and abilities as well as shortcomings. Being included in God's secrets is a humbling process because at the same time, He shares with others secrets about you and your family. Some of these you are oblivious to because of the bias toward self-justification to which we are all prone.

Finding the right local agency involves the ask/seek/ knock steps mentioned earlier. In the process you will begin to see your community in ways you never saw it before.

Family service is not a magic fix all. Sometimes we get families that contact us about volunteering who, after further investigation, are looking for a one-time experience that will somehow correct current problems in interpersonal relationships in the family, correct aberrant values in family members, or bring about sudden spiritual transformation. They want us to perform some miraculous transformation in them or their children. They expect us to somehow fix the family. These are extremely unrealistic expectations.

In fact, I would not be surprised if that initially, your family dynamics are disrupted, your relationships somewhat strained, and your spiritual life put in turmoil as a result of your family stepping out in faith to serve. You and your family are entering the realm of spiritual warfare. What you bring with you, in terms of values and attitudes, will be magnified in the pressure cooker of service. Things lying dormant will be brought to the forefront as you "stir the pot" through actively faithing in the world. This is why it is so important that you make it a point to be growing spiritually when you launch your service. It is also important that the ministry with which you work be prepared to help you and your family debrief regarding your experience of service and help you work through the spiritual issues that arise.

This is also what makes family service so exciting and rewarding. As a family you will see one another being used by God and challenged to a deeper life with Him. Having been through the same experience, yet having vastly different perceptions of that experience enables each family member to "teach" another. Each person will have something valid and unique to add to discussions about how you together saw God work and how you individually were stretched in ways you didn't anticipate. From the oldest to the youngest, each person's unique experience provides another perspective on how God is working in the world in and through your family.

Summary

God has gifted your family in amazing and unique ways. Your sensitivity to this mix of personality, age, work capacity, skills and interest will do much to make your service experience not only memorable but challenging and enjoyable. As you ask, seek and knock in prayer, God will direct you.

Short-term trips to other cultures or geographic regions may be the best way to launch a new *Mission as Life* emphasis in your family. The change in context and the challenge of a new culture provide a framework for God to work in ways not previously experienced in your lives.

Choosing an organization involves examining a number of factors that together make them ideal for helping you launch a new focus in your family. Having agencies invested in the local area assures that your families' work will have a lasting impact since the agency will build upon it once you leave. Agencies having a holistic approach will be more able to address the deep problems the families you serve experience. Having training to sensitize you to local culture and ways you may inadvertently offend locals is essential. You want to blend in as much as possible and be as effective as possible. Since you and your family will encounter challenges unfamiliar to you, it is important that the agency you select provides seasoned, well-trained mentors to work with you so that not only your questions will be answered, but your understanding spiritually and culturally about what you are experiencing will be increased. Being able to provide work suitable for all in the family is another area in which the flexibility and expertise of the agency comes to bear. You want everyone to be vitally engaged and actively serving to their capacity.

Most importantly, you want to work with an agency which will support your desire to focus your family's life on advancing God's Kingdom. You want to be sure they provide materials which will help you make *Mission as Life* a reality.

It is time to move from service as an event to service as a lifestyle.

Thank you so much for everything you guys do. I am so blessed! **My church and I are now trying to get started on working on a run down trailer park next to our church!** *I'm so excited to be able to have experienced this! David, FL*

I was much more blessed than the people we went there to bless. God is working in amazing ways through **Mustard Seeds and Mountains** *and we got to see firsthand what is happening there. Debra, FL*

Chapter 8

Thumbnail guiding principles

In the 20 plus years we have spent working with volunteers, we have learned some general principles of ministry which serve as spiritual reminders and guidelines for how not only volunteers but our own staff work together. These are kernels of wisdom which have arisen from frustrations, discouragements, spiritual warfare, and even broken hearts. They were designed to help us and our volunteers maintain perspective since the nature of our work often pulls us so deeply into people's lives that we are tempted to lose perspective in terms of how God wants to use us and how God wants to work in those we serve. These may be helpful for you and your family embarks on a life of service, especially service among the most marginalized in our society.

90% is just showing up

Nothing can happen until you put your feet on the ground. Overcoming your initial fear is often the greatest obstacle you encounter. Once that is done, and you arrive, your natural coping and adaptive mechanisms kick in and you find things to be much easier than you feared. You do have needed skills, you are able to relate to the people, and more importantly, you can see how God uses His Holy Spirit to make up for your deficiencies. Of course you don't have all the skills necessary, but with God's power you get to see what skills you do have magnified to be sufficient. Because you show up, you see God show up. Be sure when you show up that you have left your expectations behind. Too often our expectations are unrealistic. Be in the now. Allow God to use the moment to teach you and to release the gifts He has placed in you.

Anything worth doing is worth doing poorly

Some things in the world are so important that you can't wait for the expert to show up to do the job. Doing **some** thing is more effective than doing **no** thing. Our society has drilled into our heads that you must be an expert to do certain things. It's just not true. You are stronger than you think you are, you are smarter than you think you are, you are more creative than you think you are and you are tougher than you think you are. Nothing done is perfect. Do your best… that's all you can do. Do what needs to be done until you can recruit the expert to take it to the next level. Don't fall prey to the twin lie that says to do something of significance you must do something big. We put too much emphasis on the hero feat. Small things done with great love are powerful forces in people's lives. Everyone is capable of doing the small thing. What is more difficult is to keep doing the small thing with confidence that it is indeed significant. Together the drops of water form Niagara Falls.

There's only one savior and you're not Him

When you show up and begin to allow God to utilize your meager skills and abilities you begin to bond with the people. You begin to care. Sometimes it seems you begin to care for them more than they care for themselves. You want to step in and solve their problems for them. If you do, you will be disappointed because in doing so you inadvertently rob the person of their dignity and the necessity to struggle through a problem. They need to develop the strength and wisdom to avoid the same problem, or solve the same problem in the future. Sometimes you have to stop and let God be God and watch the person respond to God's work. Everything is done in God's time. When you are working with the marginalized, your heart can be broken for those you serve. You may take upon yourself a burden which God never intended for you to carry. To maintain spiritual health, to avoid burnout, to keep perspective, you have to let go, step back and reign in your desire to "save" those you serve. Your job is to assist, to introduce people to God. The saving, whether spiritual or social or economic is between them and God. There is only one Savior.

Hidden in the savior mentality is the terrible sin of pride. Those who want to save have elevated themselves to a position that should only be occupied by God. They often unknowingly are striving to make up for some deficiency within themselves, using the situation to meet some basic emotional need.

The error associated with this is often manifest in our desire to shower those we serve with gifts. There is an evil which arises from this which takes root in both the giver and the one who receives the gift. The recipient may come to see you and your family as merely a source for all the stuff they want. We have seen families become manipulative, playing mind games that foster guilt so that their greed for certain things is satiated by families who serve. We have also seen families retreat from personal service to merely giving cast off clothes, furniture or other items, being content to merely write checks as opposed to physically serving. Both reveal specific types of sin which injure both parties.

More things are done by sweat than by brilliance

Our society places too much emphasis on education. Too often we think that we can't accomplish something because we don't have specialized training or we're not smart enough. Smart is often overrated. Studies have shown that the brightest are not necessarily the most successful. More things are done by hard work than by brilliant insights. Make peace with the reality that whatever you do, if it is important or significant, it will require hard work. The easy way is an illusion. Waiting for some flash of insight is often a waste of valuable time. Step by step the longest march can be done.

A one-eyed man is king in the land of the blind

The meager knowledge you possess is often enough to start. You can learn while you go. I often tell my staff that you only have to be one step ahead of those you are serving to be their leader. In fact, your lack of expert knowledge will do much to instill in you humility. Your humble approach and willingness to learn from those you serve will make all you do more effective in the long run.

It's not who you know but who knows you

This is based upon the passage in Acts19:13-16. One must never forget that the work we do is essentially spiritual in nature, no matter how mundane or routine. One must be spiritually fit. Once you begin service you enter into the realm of spiritual warfare. You never know what you will encounter. Consequently, it is important that you practice the spiritual disciplines. You must be spiritually clean, sins confessed and seeking to live a holy life. You must be one who prays and expects God to answer. You must guard your spiritual life and cultivate your relationship with God daily. You want the evil one and his followers to fear you because of your connection and life with Christ.

If you aint dyin' you aint tryin'.

It's a good day to die. (Matthew 16:24-28) Every day of service and every act of service requires dying to self. Dying to the need for recognition or gratitude from those served, dying to ideas of fairness or personal rights. You will have new areas of selfishness, cultural insensitivity, preju-dice, personal preference revealed to you which must be put to death in order for you to allow God's Spirit to use you effectively. By learning to welcome death to issues which hinder you spiritually, you enable God to use you in ways previously unimagined while attaining ever greater levels of maturity.

You can't do some thing without some body

If I have made any grave error in my work over the years, it's starting programs without having the appropriate staff. Sometimes this principle conflicts with one of the principles above. You can get overcommitted. You can stretch yourself to the point where what you do is ineffective. Over commit-ment creeps into other areas of your life and sabotages other activities. You may see the need, but now may not be the time to meet it. Now may be the time to pray that the Lord send out laborers into the harvest.

The smallest can be the biggest

Our society emphasizes the hero feat. We think that to do something significant one must found an organization, launch a movement, or give a million dollars. That is a lie from the evil one designed to stop us in our tracks. Doing small things with great love is the foundation of our work. Everyone can do small things. Everyone has the power to love. In fact, each person has an inexhaustible capacity to love and receive love. Small acts are magnified into gigantic proportions when permeated with great love. Love never fails.

God never rushes you except when He's in a hurry

It is tempting to try to rush to get as much done as possible. It fits in with the idea that somehow we must save this situation or these people. Whenever I begin to feel undue pressure to purchase something, build something, initiate a new program, I come back to this principle. God lives in eternity. Everything to Him is in the eternal now. Look at how He has dealt with people. It took 400 years of prayer for Him to release the Israelites from bondage in Egypt. It took over 21 years for Him to deliver Joseph from being unjustly imprisoned. God's time is different from ours. We tend to be impatient. In rare instances do you see God moving quickly, such as with Philip and the Ethiopian Eunuch. God sometimes rushes when salvation is involved, but for the most part He moves methodically. Give time for God to work in people's lives.

The greater the risk you take, the more you forsake, the greater God's Kingdom you make

You cannot serve God without taking risks. The lessons of faith never end. God likes those who attempt great things for Him because it reveals great trust in Him. You can do more than you think you can. How creative and daring can you become when seeking to advance the Kingdom of God?

Summary

You and your family are embarking on an amazing journey. Prepare to have your lives altered in exciting ways. The principles above serve as guidelines. You will find yourselves tempted with each of the areas mentioned and then some more too.

The principles exist to help you run the race to the end. You are in a marathon, not a sprint. You must develop a long haul mentality. Incremental change over time is like compound interest, the longer it works the more powerful and astonishing it becomes.

Once you begin your journey of service and have some time under your belts, take time to write out your story. Go to the *Mission as Life* website and post your story so others can be encouraged and get ideas on how they can serve. How did you overcome your fears? What impact did the service have on you and your family? How do you and your family see the world differently now? What kinds of changes have you made in your lifestyle and how did it initially affect you? Share the new levels of commitment in terms of time, treasure and talents your family has attained. Your family and your story are important. Share with others and recruit friends.

Social change begins with personal change. The changes you make personally, the changes your family makes affect others. I believe the winsomeness and sense of purpose you and your family will project to friends will be attractive. I believe there are thousands of people and families out there who are just waiting for something to become involved in which is greater than themselves and their personal concerns. They intuitively know that they were made for more than what they are currently doing. Together, you and your family, me and my family, can model another way to live. A way that will eventually make this world in which we live a better place to live; a way that honors the Lamb that was slain from the foundation of the world and wins for Him the fruit of His suffering.

What are you waiting for?

References

1. Research, B. (2004) Only half of protestant pastors have a Biblical worldview. 1/15/2004

2. Barna, G., Revolutionary parenting. What the research shows really works. 2007, Carol Stream, IL : Tyndale House. 167

3. Voddie Baucham, J., *Family driven faith: Do what it takes to raise sons and daughters who walk with God.* 2007, Wheaton, IL: Crossway Books. 218

4. Guinness, O., *Fit bodies fat minds: Why Evangelicals don't think and what to do about it.,* 1994, Grand Rapids, MI. Baker Books.

5. Guinness, O. and J. Seel, *No god but God: Breaking with the idols of our age. 1992, Chicago,* Moody Press.

6. Moll, R., Scrooge lives! Why we are not putting more in the offering plate, and what we can do about it., in Christianity Today. 2008, Christianity Today International: Carol Stream, IL p. 24-29

Resources

Mission as Life web page www.missionaslife. com

This is a place for you:

To read about what kinds of creative things other families are doing to promote a God-centered lifestyle in their home.

To find resources for educating yourself regarding missions in general. This includes materials especially geared for working with children. This includes links to other web pages and a *Mission as Life* store.

To discover mission agencies that strive to make short-term trips more than a feel good experience, but rather a launching point for the development of life-long service right where families currently live.

For churches to come to discover how they can help families develop lifestyles of service in not only missions but community life.

For mission agencies to come to learn how they can alter what they do to become more family friendly for volunteers, and how to promote a *Mission as Life* lifestyle with their volunteers.

To find Mission as Life events where you can discover *Mission as Life* speakers in your area, fundraisers, or Mission as Life gatherings.

Take a look at our Mission as Life facebook group.
http://www.facebook.com/home.php#/group.php?gid=54907503020

Mustard Seeds and Mountains web page www.mustardseeds.org provides opportunities for serving the poor in Appalachia.

Its facebook group, Friends of Mustard Seeds and Mountains, http://www.facebook.com/home.php#!/group.php?gid=70096661981, is a place where you can keep up with what God is doing in the lives of those who volunteer with them and learn about how they are trying to serve at home.

Books on Mission for Families
52 ways to teach missions to kids

These crafts, games, and outreaches will help your students become more involved with your church's missionaries while also helping your kids become missionaries in their own neighborhoods. Missions are not a matter of choice; they are an act of obedience to Christ. The missionaries of tomorrow are the 4-12 year old children of today. The 52 exciting activities in this book teach the concept and importance of missions to your children. It will also involve children in supporting missionaries through their prayers, interest, financial giving and service.

Author: Nancy S. Williamson

Families on mission: Ideas for teaching your preschooler to love, share, and care

Families on Mission is a book of fun family activity ideas that will help parents teach their preschoolers how to love, share, and care about others. Parents today must compete with many other influences that shape their preschool child's life. That's why it is important for parents to begin early to teach Christian values and beliefs to their child. Packed with creative ideas, this book will help parents discover ways to involve their preschoolers in ministry activities designed just for their small hands. These creative projects and activities, which are easy to do and require few resources, create family models for praying for others, helping others, and becoming active in the community.

Author: Angie Quantrell

The Mission-minded family: Releasing your family to God's destiny

In a mission-minded family, there's a God-infused energy. There's a focus on God's worldwide purpose and there's a passion for the lost. There's a spiritual depth and hunger that reaches beyond the maintenance mode of cultural Christianity. A mission-minded family emphasizes leadership, calling and destiny. There's a prevailing attitude of self-sacrifice and an emphasis on total submission to God's will. There's an unmistakable and contagious joy. Dunagan, who wrote *The Mission-Minded Child*, brings the same perspective to what it means to be a mission-minded family. This book includes suggested activities for families to participate in together as well as resources to help families develop the desire to be more missions-focused. She discusses the need for families to balance and prioritize their everyday lives and delves into what a family's finances would look like if they were focused on missions. This practical book is the perfect companion to *The Mission-Minded Child*. Families who read and practice principles from this book will receive a rekindled closeness as they participate in ministry together.

Author: Ann Dunagan

Missions moments 2: 52 easy to use missional messages & activities for today's family

In *Missions Moments 2*, mother and children's missions education expert provides parents with an easy-to-use teaching resource. A convenient tool to guide parents as they help their children develop a proper biblical worldview, parents will find 52 weeks of 5- minute missions messages paired with a 15-minute application activity for children. Each lesson is written in a simple style so that messages can be adapted to children's ages, maturity levels, etc. A Bible verse to memorize is also included for each week. There's a challenging "Make It Home" section that provides ideas for how to incorporate the week's message into the life of the whole family. Ideal for parents of elementary school-age children, *Missions Moments 2* will bring families together around God's call to be the light of the world.

Author: Mitzi Eaker

Christian heroes then and now

YWAM Publishing. These exciting, challenging, and deeply touching true stories chronicle the lives of ordinary men and women whose trust in God accomplished extraordinary exploits for His kingdom and glory. Written specifically to challenge readers with the powerful lives of missionaries who have profoundly shaped history, these books answer today's call for positive role models and for opportunities to see how God works through the lives of those who follow him. The exciting life stories of these heroes will inspire the readers as they witness the drama of faith and character being tested under the most extreme circumstances.

http://www.ywampublishing.com/p-470-christian-heroes-then-nowbrcomplete-set-books-1-34.aspx

Books on Mission Vision and Reaching Unreached People Groups
God's heart for the nations

God's Heart for the Nations rips apart old understandings of God's plan and purpose for our lives. In eight lessons, author and global activist Jeff Lewis probes for the heart and mind of God as he combines powerful Bible passages with challenging and provocative questions. Each lesson is followed by a time of meditation and a focus on an unreached people group. If you really knew the heart and mind of God, would you dare to follow Him?

Author: Jeff Lewis

Operation world

The updated version of this remarkable prayer encyclopedia tells what God has been doing in numerous countries. Factual and very detailed, *Operation World* is also inspiring in its coverage of the powerful reality of God's Spirit at work around the world.

Author: Patrick Johnstone & Jason Mandryk

Serving as senders

The title says it all! A missionary needs care in at least six areas: Moral Support, Logistics Support, Financial Support, Prayer Support, Communication Support, and Reentry Support. This book gives scores of practical ideas on how a team can provide the necessary care for a missionary. Chapter One tells "when" and "why" a missionary needs care. Chapters Two through Seven deal with each of the six areas of care. Chapter Eight brings it back to the individual's involvement in care-giving.

Author: Neal Pirolo

Books on Cultural Adjustment or Sensitivity
Re-Entry: Making the transition from mission life to life at home

In his dedication, the author states, "This book is written for those about to go into missions, for those who currently are in missions, and for those who were in missions and have experienced the challenges of re-entry." A very practical book that will help with some of the difficulties of returning.

Author: Peter Jordan

Barnga: A simulation game on cultural clashes (25th Anniversary Edition) Revised and expanded for it's 25th Anniversary, Barnga is the classic simulation game on cultural clashes. Participants experience the shock of realizing that despite their good intentions and the many similarities amongst themselves, people interpret things differently from one another in profound ways, especially people from differing cultures. Players learn that they must understand and reconcile these differences if they want to function effectively in a cross-cultural group.

Author: Sivasailam Thiagarajan, Raja Thiagarajan

Books on Poverty
A Framework for understanding poverty

People in poverty face challenges virtually unknown to those in middle class or wealth—challenges from both obvious and hidden sources. The reality of being poor brings out a survival mentality, and turns attention away from opportunities taken for granted by everyone else. If you work with people from poverty, some understanding of how different their world is from yours will be invaluable. Whether you're an educator—or a social, health, or legal services professional—this breakthrough book gives you practical, real-world support and guidance to improve your effectiveness in working with people from all socioeconomic backgrounds.

Since 1995 *A Framework for Understanding Poverty* has guided hundreds of thousands of educators and other professionals through the pitfalls and barriers faced by all classes, especially the poor. Carefully researched and packed with charts, tables, and questionnaires, Framework not only documents the facts of poverty, it provides practical yet compassionate strategies for addressing its impact on people's lives.
Author: Ruby K. Payne

Poverty in America: A handbook
In a remarkably concise, readable, and accessible format, John Iceland provides a comprehensive picture of poverty in America. He shows how poverty is measured and understood and how it has changed over time, as well as how public policies have grappled with poverty as a political issue and an economic reality. This edition has been updated and includes a new preface.
Author: John Iceland

Cry of the Urban Poor: Reaching the slums of today's megacities
Viv Grigg is known around the globe as a prophetic voice calling Christians to follow Christ into the squatter areas of the developing world—where few churches exist. In this revised edition of *Cry of the Urban Poor*, Grigg uses updated statistics and information to describe the economic and spiritual needs of the world's poorest city slums.
Author: Viv Grigg

Working with the Poor: New insights and learnings from development practitioners
Here development practitioners from around the world struggle to overcome the Western assumption that the physical and spiritual realms are separate and distinct from one another in answering the question *How do Christian prac-*

titioners express holistic transformational development authentically?
Bryant Myers, editor

Companion to the Poor: Christ in the urban slums
A challenge to reexamine our strategies and design new approaches that will build Christ's Kingdom among the poor, who comprise half the world.
Author: Viv Grigg

When helping hurts: Alleviating poverty without hurting the poor and ourselves
Churches and individual Christians typically have faulty assumptions about the causes of poverty, resulting in the use of strategies that do considerable harm to poor people and themselves. *When Helping Hurts* provides foundational concepts, clearly articulated general principles and relevant applications. The result is an effective and holistic ministry to the poor, not a truncated gospel.
Authors: Brian Fikkert and Steve Corbett

Books on the Kingdom of God
The upside-down kingdom
This revised and updated version of the classic, originally published in 1978, is an intriguing study of the Kingdom of God in the Gospels. Reflecting the latest insights from recent New Testament scholarship, it demonstrates the sociological perspective's creative ability to uncover new meaning in old biblical texts. Kraybill says social, religious and economic practices of the dominant culture usually favor the rich, powerful, prestigious. Jesus, on the other hand, favors those who suffer at society's margins and fall between the cracks.
Author: Kraybill, D. B. (1978).

The Kingdom manifesto: Calling the church to live under God's reign.

Everywhere the church is rediscovering Jesus' call to live under God's rule. How can the church stabilize families, revitalize neighborhoods and create a just and peaceful world? Snyder takes you on a focused look at the Kingdom of God and how living its principles helps answer the above questions.

Author: Snyder, H. A. (1985).

The magnificent obsession

Jesus commands us to seek first the Kingdom of God. But, what is the Kingdom of God? Swartz takes you on a journey that helps you see that the Kingdom of God is a magnificent obsession which imbues its followers with passion, mystery, revolution and power. He challenges us to take up the challenge of the Kingdom, making the pursuit of it central in our lives.

Author: Swartz, D. (1990).

Jesus mean and wild

Many Christians are used to the idea of a meek and mild Jesus, the stereotypical "nice guy." Countering these all too prevalent notions, Mark Galli offers a unique study of seventeen troubling passages from the Gospel of Mark to prove we should be anything but comfortable with Christ. Highlighting the undeniable fact of an untamable and often militant Messiah, Galli gives readers a training manual in spiritual growth to awaken sleeping believers and transform them into devoted disciples. Hinging on the compelling nature of the love of God, he explains how this mean and wild Jesus shows us truer love than our pleasant construct ever could. Striking and bold, always rooted in Scripture, *Jesus Mean and Wild* will put readers on the road to true discipleship.

Author: Galli, M. (2006).

Rediscovering the Kingdom

From the very beginning God's plan for His creation was centered on our being in relationship with Him. It was never God's plan to establish a religion. This is "the book" for "the hour" in which we live and will take us back to the beginning of all things where we will discover God's original intention for humankind.

Author: Myles Monroe

Web pages to help with family mission growth.

Global Xpress Kids Club http://www.globalxpresskc.com/ Kids can join a *Mailbox Club* and get regular packets of material which help them learn of missions around the world and how children around the world live. They provide an *Xpress Sunday School* program to teach missions in churches as well as produce an *Xpress Lil Engine Magazine* which monthly takes kids to various countries, learning about the culture and people and about what God is doing there.

Wonder Zone http://www.wonderzone.com/ An interactive site by Child Evangelism Fellowship that has activities, games, adventure stories and Bible stories for kids. Set up for kids to navigate easily.

NTM Kidstuff http://www.ntm.org/kidstuff/ Read missionary stories and play the games that go with them. You'll discover it's fun — and easy — to be part of God's plan to take the Gospel to the ends of the earth.

SIM Kids http://www.simkids.org/ An interactive site where kids can play games, learn about missions in various countries, write kids in other countries, and read stories.

Wycliffe Kids Web http://www.wycliffe.org/kids/ An interactive web site where kids learn of mission work going on in the world, learn of other cultures, and play games.

One Hen http://www.onehen.org A website that teaches kids about microfinance and how it is used around the world to assist in alleviating poverty. Interactive games and stories along with ways children can make a difference internationally.